PRAISE FOR *SPIRIT HUNGER*

Using her own personal story and experiences, Gari Meacham relates to women of all ages and backgrounds. She understands our hunger to be intimately connected to God and our confusing tendencies to fill that deep yearning apart from him. In *Spirit Hunger*, Gari shares insights into prayer, faith, and belief that lead us toward an authentic love of God.

—DR. ED YOUNG, senior pastor,
Second Baptist Church, Houston, Texas

In sharing struggles as well as triumphs, Gari Meacham ultimately shows us a new understanding of prayer — not just the worrying kind, but authentic, powerful communication. *Spirit Hunger* invites us to enter into a whole new relationship with our Lord.

—#1 *New York Times* bestselling author DEBBIE MACOMBER

Gari Meacham has personally wrestled with the very things that cause a person's deep Spirit hunger. Gari is not writing from textbook research but life's classroom. *Spirit Hunger* contains principles that have been carefully mined from God's Word. Each chapter provides such insight that the reader's spiritual hunger pangs will be satisfied. As the Spirit hunger is satisfied, one's soul will soar to new heights.

—JACKIE KENDALL, bestselling author of *Lady in Waiting*
and president of Power to Grow

GARI MEACHAM

spirit hunger

FILLING OUR DEEP LONGING

TO CONNECT WITH GOD

ZONDERVAN®

ZONDERVAN.com/
AUTHORTRACKER
follow your favorite authors

ZONDERVAN

Spirit Hunger
Copyright © 2012 by Gari Meacham

This title is also available as a Zondervan ebook. Visit www.zondervan.com/ebooks.

This title is also available in a Zondervan audio edition. Visit www.zondervan.fm.

Requests for information should be addressed to:

Zondervan, *Grand Rapids, Michigan 49530*

Library of Congress Cataloging-in-Publication Data

Meacham, Gari.
    Spirit hunger : filling our deep longing to connect with God / Gari Meacham.
      p. cm.
    Includes bibliographical references
    ISBN 978-0-310-30900-0
    1. Spirituality. I. Title.
  BV4501.3.M425 2012
  248.4—dc23   2012010596

Published in association with the Books & Such Literary Agency, 52 Mission Circle, Suite 122, PMB 170, Santa Rosa, CA 95409-5370, www.booksandsuch.com.

Cover design: Greg Jackson /Thinkpen Design
Cover photography: Shutterstock®
Interior illustration: © 2012 Paul June
Interior design: Katherine Lloyd /The DESK

Printed in the United States of America

12 13 14 15 16 17 /DCI/ 23 22 21 20 19 18 17 16 15 14 13 12 11 10 9 8 7 6 5 4 3 2 1

The author who benefits you most is not the one
who tells you something you did not know before,
but the one who gives expression to the truth that
has been dumbly struggling in you for utterance.

Oswald Chambers

To the authors who have walked before me . . .
inspiring me to dumbly struggle

CONTENTS

part one: a heart that longs

part two: a heart that seeks

part three: a heart that moves

ACKNOWLEDGMENTS

I love reading authors' acknowledgments because I know that writing a book is much harder than it looks. It is a task that rivals childbirth, and the pains of my labor have been exceedingly helped by those I want to thank.

To Bobby — lover of my soul — I thank you for the countless talks and prayer and for the courage you exude that lets me tell your stories as well as my own.

To my children, Brooke, Ally, and Colton; my son-in-law, Maurice; and my grandbaby, Reese — you are my joy and crown. I thank God for teaching me so much through you. I adore you.

To my mom, sister, brother, dad, and grandparents — you are the bright mosaic of my life. I love you more than words can express.

To my dear friend Leanne Jamieson and the women of Second Baptist Church in Houston — thank you for taking this journey with me and letting me explore this material with you.

To my editors John Sloan and Dirk Buursma — you have taught me and mentored me with grace and encouragement. Thanks for your kindred spirit toward this work, and thanks for your gentle hand that led me through the pages.

To Cindy Lambert, Don Gates, Karin Tyrer, Robin Phillips, and the entire team at Zondervan — each hand this book has passed through has touched it with excellence. My thanks to you.

To the Zondervan DVD and curriculum team — thanks for your vision and cheerleading.

To Wendy Lawton, my agent and friend — thanks for speaking the words "for such a time as this ..." over my life.

To my former students at Peabody Elementary School — I think I learned most of what I know about writing from you.

To the people who work at Panera Bread — you always greeted me with a friendly smile and a large cup for me to fill with iced tea. I'm grateful.

To my friends in Major League Baseball — it is an honor to be part of this wonderful game with you all.

Finally, and most important — I thank my Savior, Jesus, who has saved, inspired, and rearranged my life. Without him I have no story to tell ...

PART ONE

a heart that longs

chapter 1

—

SIGHS OF
A HUNGRY SPIRIT

One day, I stumbled across some words David wrote in the book of Psalms. My mouth dropped open as I absorbed his tone, and a quiet sigh settled over the stained patio furniture I was sitting on as I read:

> O God, You are my God; I shall seek You earnestly,
> My soul thirsts for You, my flesh yearns for You,
> In a dry and weary land where there is no water.
>
> Psalm 63:1 NASB

David's words called out to me, speaking to me from the depth of his pain. A spiritual pain. He is hungry for the God he knows intimately. His flesh yearns for him in a land that doesn't understand.

This rattled me and got me thinking. How would I revise this psalm based on my life today? It might sound a little like this:

O God, You are my God; I shall try to see You in my day if I have
*   time,*
But if I don't, You know I am winking at You.
My soul thirsts for Diet Cokes, lattes, and sweet tea.
I'm not really sure what thirsting for You looks like.
My flesh yearns to be beautiful, in shape, fat free.
My flesh yearns for acceptance and accolades, an insatiable
*   need for cheerleading.*
There's a lot of water in my life — bottled, sparkling, and lemon
*   spritzed,*
But I don't often drink it.
I like it, but I'm not weary over needing it.

The stark difference in these versions slapped me across the face. It has haunted me and prodded me to write this book. I believe there is a deep place of engaging God — of needing him, wanting him, and enjoying him. I don't want to be a committed Christian; I want to be a desperate Christian.

Are we experiencing this longing and desperation throughout our days, or are we mildly satisfied with life? Crying out when things get tough, and then settling back into a marginal understanding and compliance with a predictable Christ? We are built for a Spirit hunger. Designed to thirst for a God who quenches. So why do we settle for crumbs under the table like dogs?

Part of our settling circles back to an iconic message that we've either heard or uttered at some point in our lives: "This is the best it's going to get; I better get used to it."

A woman I met was sharing how she felt trapped in her marriage. She was a writer, and after a profound encounter with God, she wanted to pen a book titled *Trapped in a Bad Marriage? Paint the Cage Gold!* Although I love this title, it's not a clear picture of what God invites us to. We're invited to so much more than a golden cage.

I've always been a bit awkward at romance. The first boy who ever

caught my eye was Tom Kerr. He was a blond-haired, blue-eyed trou-blemaker, and all the girls in third grade were crazy about him.

On the days when our teacher changed the seating arrangement, I swear you could hear silent prayers being offered: "Please let me end up in Tom's row!" My problem was that although I did get those coveted seats a few times that year, I was just coming off a two-year stint in remedial pullouts because I struggled in reading and math. "OK, God," I bargained, "maybe in a year or two I'll be popular enough to get a look from Tom."

In fifth grade my dream finally came true. Through the grapevine of grade school notes and whispers, I learned that Tom Kerr liked me!

It happened on the night of the fifth grade musical. He took a black onyx ring that had a diamond in the center (a *glass* diamond) and threw it at me on the playground before the show. No words were exchanged, but the throw was tender.

That single event changed the course of our entire fifth grade class. Boys were throwing rings at girls left and right. There were no conver-sations, but a lot of ring-wearing fifth graders who declared themselves "going steady."

This silly encounter reminds me of faith today. We've got the rings on, but we have no idea how to engage the ring giver.

Could it be that we long for a romance with God — but we're too tired, wounded, realistic, or skeptical to accept one? Back when John and Stasi Eldredge wrote their *New York Times* bestseller *Captivating*, I bought it, but I couldn't read it.[1] As a matter of fact, I lost it and had to buy another copy — yet I was still not compelled to turn a page. It was as if I knew I had a deep longing for romance with God, but to unlock that Pandora's Box only meant I would go to a place of touchy-feely disappointment. Besides, I was busy serving God. Romance is a luxury. It's a negligee when I'd rather wear a T-shirt. A rose when I feel like a dandelion. A soufflé instead of a hot dog.

What I didn't realize was that I was already in a romance with God. It wasn't defined with starry words penned by Hallmark but had the

sweet echo of phrases like "bride of Christ, Lover of my soul, and the One who won't forget."

I once heard John Eldredge, the same author I couldn't bear to read, state, "A woman is made to have a life-offering, captivating effect on those around her. A tender lover with the strength to invite to something of God."

How can I be a tender lover — inviting those I know to a glimpse of romance that defies routine days and the insecurity that accompanies it?

As women we've been taught from the crib that it's up to us to woo a lover. Be a good girl for Daddy. Sit up straight, brush your hair, and act sweet. Clean your plate, but don't get fat. Hide the very core of who you are because if that is exposed, a lover will run.

Men seem as confused about romance as women are. Pursue, but don't smother. Be brave, but be tender, act sweet, but stand like a man. Before we know it, we've buried our longings for our Creator underneath a stack of compliance, confusion, and duty. What we know of romance with God is either measured by the heartbreaks we've endured from lovers or relegated to the pages of our own bland history in which we've tried to find God.

The difference is that "God romance" isn't boring, risky, or stale. It doesn't stink or have bad breath in the morning. *He woos us.* He goes after us. He strongly pursues us with a melody and a longing for intimate love. Not the kind of love we know with our finite minds and suspicious hearts, but a love that transcends hope and logic. This longing gives birth to desire — and the romance of God wells up out of who we are.

What Do We Long For?

Some longings seem to come forth from deep within. Most psychologists and sociologists agree that certain longings are universal, beginning at birth and carried through till we take our last breath. We long for

nurturing, attention, and affirmation; we long for filling and purpose; we long for intimacy — to hear and be heard; we long for discipline.

In my years of teaching elementary school, I saw the need for nurture, attention, and affirmation play out daily in the confines of my classroom. I taught with the unspoken motto, "Make every child feel like they're your favorite." I knew if I could convince them I loved them, they would break their backs for me. In fifteen years of teaching it never failed. Never. Some years I felt like an Oscar-winning actress portraying my love — but it never failed.

One little boy will forever be a scar on my heart. Sammy was a lost child in a brood of five kids.[*] His mother up and walked out on the dad and her small children. By the time I got him in third grade, his agony and grief were bleeding all over his life. "Failing in school, multiple suspensions, and dark moods" was how his academic life was described in the report I received when he entered my room in August. He was irritating too. Moody, mean, lazy — and that was on a good day!

The special education teacher and I shared a love for God and the audacity to believe more for Sammy, so we decided to meet every Monday and discuss his goals, as well as to pray for him. As the year progressed, I noticed that whenever Sammy was asked to draw something, it was violent, bloody, and dark. I pulled him aside and explained that he was loved by God and that light, goodness, and hope could fill his darkness. It was a gutsy move to make in the public school system, but this kid was sinking fast, and I knew if I didn't hand him a life jacket, he would drown.

Soon I began to see his drawings take on new light. Happy people, the sun, and bright colors replaced blood and guts. It was a start.

Instead of penalizing him for not turning in his homework, I decided to offer the gift of my time to Sammy so we could close the gaping hole in his education. We stayed after school together and got his homework done. I listened to him read, and when projects were

---

[*] The boy's name has been changed in this story.

due, he had something to turn in. But the greatest affirmation of his longings leaked out at the end of the school year when I invited him to a summer Bible study at my home. My own son, Colton, was Sammy's age, so we invited six boys to our home for an informal gathering to hear some good news. I drove to Sammy's disheveled house to pick him up. I don't think anyone even noticed he left with me or asked about when he might return.

Toward the end of our time together, we gathered knee to knee, sitting Indian style on the carpet in our family room to pray. Each boy was asked what was going on in his life and what he wanted to talk to God about. With a wild look in his eyes that signaled a geyser was about to erupt, Sammy uncharacteristically burst into tears and wailed, "My mom left, and it's my fault. If I behaved better, she would still love us!"

I came undone — and each nine-year-old boy in that room shook his head as young boys do when they have no words to say. We cradled him, and I whispered into his dirty hair, "You are loved. You are not to blame," as we rocked back and forth in raw shame and heartache. His need for nurture, attention, and affirmation was bellowing from him like the sobs from his chest and mine.

I wish I could say I still have a relationship with Sammy, and that all is well after all these years. The truth is, I don't know what happened to him after he left our school. I heard that his older brother ended up in prison, but that Sammy was trying to stay on track and graduate. I can only hope his longings have been filled by his attentive Father in heaven. Unlike a faltering mother or an inattentive dad, he has a Father who fills to capacity and then spills some more.

We Long for Purpose

I once heard a story about a group of Jews who survived the Holocaust. Placed in a work camp, they were part of an experiment on human nature. The Jews in one part of the camp were given jobs to complete that required teamwork and planning. They were asked to move timber and rocks from one corner of the camp to another and then to organize the rubble in a neat fashion. Even the children and older detainees were involved in the work, transferring small sticks and clearing new pathways. Once that job was complete, another menial job was assigned to them. The results were astonishing, as every member who was part of the work force survived, while other members of the same camp who wandered around aimlessly each day died.

We are created for purpose. Designed to matter. Without purpose, we wobble about in inactivity and indifference, hosting a stale, tasteless outlook on life.

My husband, Bobby, and I have been involved in professional baseball for over thirty years. Stadiums can be found across the country, both in remote minor-league towns that house splintering bench seats out in center field and in bustling cities where brand-new parks are common. In all of them, we've watched a curious pattern of behavior. The fans who seem to enjoy themselves the most are those who feel they matter to the team. Faces painted, signs scribbled on poster board and waved frantically in the air — they feel that their presence and contribution to the game help determine its outcome.

Marla was a season ticket holder in a desert town named Rancho Cucamonga. Positioned between overshadowing mountains and plains of swaying palm trees, this city housed a minor-league team for the California Angels. The team's name was the Quakes (yes, after earthquakes!), and our mascots wore jerseys with the names Tremor and Aftershock proudly embroidered on the backs. Just the mention of these names sent this Colorado girl into a state of panic.

Bobby managed the team, and each night I watched as Marla unpacked her scorebook, cowbell, and Quakes pennant to wave wildly from the stands. One night, Marla nestled up next to me, lamenting that she had to miss the game the next night. I looked at her quizzically as if to say, "What's the big deal?"

Marla looked me square in the eye and said, "I feel like if I'm not here cheering, the team may lose. They need me!"

Strange as it may seem, this comment delighted me. I don't know what else was going on in Marla's life, but when the Quakes were in town, she felt like she mattered. Her purpose was to cheer the team on to victory, and I believe this purpose filled her longing to matter, even if it only resonated with quirky mascots and the fans she called friends.

When my three kids graduated from high school and left home, although I was swamped with my own career and aspirations and my husband's insane baseball schedule, I stumbled around for a year with an empty feeling in my stomach. My social circle changed, my schedule changed, my focus changed — and a giant piece of my purpose for the last twenty years broke off like an iceberg detaching from a glacier.

The same thing happens when we leave a job to raise kids, move from a place we love to follow a spouse's paycheck, or leave behind the life of a single to join ourselves to a husband. Our longing for purpose overshadows every other need — and sometimes it needs to be redefined and re-created. We're built to feel like we matter.

I finally decided to allow myself those times of tears as I walked from empty room to empty room of the house and sat on beds no longer slept in. I began to welcome the quiet and peace, while allowing God to re-create a new sense of purpose. I could finally slyly mutter, "At least these empty rooms stay clean!"

We Long for Intimacy — To Hear and Be Heard

Children have an uncanny way of blasting through our smoke screens. When our oldest daughter, Brooke, was a toddler, she would take hold of my face and turn it to hers if she was trying to tell me a story while I was multitasking. With sticky fingers and marbled words she would say, "Mommy, why are you not listening to me?"

Even children know when they aren't being heard. Nothing burns like the sting of our voices being stifled, shut out, or ignored. I have to admit that I haven't always been the best listener. A few years ago, Bobby mentioned that he didn't think I paid attention when he was speaking to me. I'm embarrassed to say my response was, "Huh? What did you say? I wasn't listening!"

Since then, I've committed to tuning in. I no longer nod without the decency of hearing what I'm responding to. Whether it's our husband, friends, children, or bosses — we long to be listened to, even if we have to turn a chin to ensure that we're being heard.

We Long for Discipline

At first glance, you may think this concept doesn't belong in a list of longings. To some women, *discipline* is just shy of a cussword — dirty, nasty, and something we try for but never attain. The truth is, we long for it. We're built for it. Consider Paul's words to the men and women in Galatia: "The fruit of the Spirit is love, joy, peace, patience, kindness, goodness, faithfulness, gentleness, self-control; against such things there is no law" (Galatians 5:22 – 23 NASB).

Sitting smack in the middle of such flowery words as *love*, *joy*, *peace*, and *patience* is the word *self-control*. It reeks of weed killer in a meadow of wildflowers.

We know we long for discipline when we've languished in laziness, procrastination, or disobedience and it no longer feels like we're getting away with something. Bingeing, sleeping in, missing deadlines, ignoring time with God, or lying around with our house in disarray ends up feeling lousy. It runs counter to the rhythms of our deepest longings.

If discipline is something we long for, why does it smell like mildewed laundry? In my life I have fought with discipline as if it were a pesky gnat, swatting at it as though I can bring it under control. Everything in place, everyone behaving nicely — eat perfect, dress perfect, smile perfect. Discipline becomes the taskmaster and whip that march me onto the stage of fake excellence.

Once I tire of the harsh boundaries of discipline, I toy with the spacious boundaries of indulgence. More food, more pleasure, more stuff. Somewhere between perfection and indulgence lies the outline of grace. Grace is both the permission to not be perfect and the invitation to leave self-gratification behind. Discipline blooms when we live in this gracious balance.

This leads to a basic question that begs an answer. If we're built with these longings and desires, how did things get so messed up? When did desires turn to hauntings? If we're created to long, what happens when longings languish in an evaporating pool of hope?

The answer lies in the fundamental relationship God had with Eve and Adam. I know it seems like this topic has been beaten to a pulp in church circles, but what we think we know from this story truly doesn't match what we should glean from it. If we had learned our lessons, men would treat women much differently than they do, and women would view themselves in a far better light.[2]

chapter 2

—

FIGHTING THE DRAGON WITH A TOOTHPICK

W hen God began creating, he took darkness and turned it to light. Void turned to matter. Air, water, stars, moons, expanses hummed to his tune. But he longed for more. He longed for an image bearer who would be a reflection of him like a child mirrors his father. God longed for the intimacy of a creator and the created. So he formed man and breathed the breath of life into him.

You'd think that would have been enough, but God still had one final gesture of love. A last bit of chocolate frosting to put on the cake, a polished gem to crown his jewelry box of creation. That gem was woman. Like a painting with perfect hues, so is the masterpiece of man and woman.

Eve's and Adam's lives consisted of relishing the fruit of God's creation, a titillating romance with mates who gazed only at one another, and an exclusive engagement with their creator — their God. Nothing should have competed with this kind of glory … but it did. We hear it called *the fall of man*, but I'd like to rename it *the devastation of woman*.

Most of the women I know don't feel like special icing on a cake or a gem in a jewelry box. I've asked around, and most women see themselves as tired, worn-out, used-up, undisciplined in some areas and overly disciplined in others, unsexy, isolated, and insecure. A far cry from the image of womanhood described in the language of Genesis.

The fact that Eve was approached by Satan isn't surprising; after all, we are the trusting type. Eager to please and make Daddy proud. The serpent was no dummy as he went straight for the woman's jugular with his rancid deception:

Now the serpent was more crafty than any of the wild animals the LORD God had made. He said to the woman, "Did God really say, 'You must not eat from any tree in the garden'?"

The woman said to the serpent, "We may eat fruit from the trees in the garden, but God did say, 'You must not eat fruit from the tree that is in the middle of the garden, and you must not touch it, or you will die.'"

"You will not certainly die," the serpent said to the woman. "For God knows that when you eat from it your eyes will be opened, and you will be like God, knowing good and evil."

When the woman saw that the fruit of the tree was good for food and pleasing to the eye, and also desirable for gaining wisdom, she took some and ate it. She also gave some to her husband, who was with her, and he ate it.

Genesis 3:1 – 6

Up to this point, Eve's longings and desires matched her life. Loving husband, physical needs cared for, physical appearance appreciated and enjoyed (they were constantly naked, for goodness' sake!), and a communion with her Creator that was vibrant and real. But the jugular Satan targeted to get Eve's attention heard the whispered, "Yes, it *does* get better than that. God is holding out on you."

Eve acknowledged the one protective rule that God laid over their lives: "Don't mess with the tree in the middle of the garden. It's got a knowledge to it that will shred your heart."

She knew it meant death — the death of innocence — and Satan pounced on her knowledge with a lie so handsomely deceitful it sounded right. "You surely won't die! God knows you'll be more like him if you eat from this tree — and that's a good thing."

What happens next is both fascinating and heartbreaking because it defines the way women embrace life to this day. After she ate the fruit, she took it upon herself to convince her husband that he needed to follow her. That she knew what was best for him.

The Bible doesn't give a time frame for how long it took Eve to get Adam to eat from the same tree, but I have a hunch it may not have been immediate. I think she wore him down. Nagging him relentlessly, and then possibly coyly crying out, "Don't you love me? Don't you want to do what I've done and stay close to me?"

I'm smiling as I write this because I can think of countless times I've figured out how to get my way with Bobby and still make him think he's the man! Because I'm a strong-willed, independent, mustang type of woman, reining me in has always been a bit of a challenge. I'm usually most pliable after I've run myself into a two-by-four trying to create the world according to me, and then maybe I'll allow the protective arms of my husband to wrap around me like a quilt. Prior to "the devastation of woman," the word *control* had never been uttered. Now it is screaming from the treetops.

Adam did the most dangerous thing imaginable. In the midst of the crying and convincing, he kept silent. He didn't protect or fight for her; he just went limp … and all hell quietly broke loose. Their initial experience of living and loving in a Spirit hunger relationship with God was shattered.

COWARDS AND CONTROLLERS

Adam wasn't born a baby. His needs were covered in terms of sleep, food, warmth, and fellowship with his Father. But God longed to nurture

Adam in a more intimate way by giving him Eve. Unfortunately, Adam chose silence, and Eve chose control. The more a man is silent, the more a woman pushes for control. It's a vicious cycle that can beat itself raw.

I've spent many years believing I wasn't the controlling type, only to discover that to some degree, we all are. My friend Cindy said it perfectly: "Women are either controlling or being controlled." Control is a thorn that continues to pierce our hearts, and it's the wise woman who tackles the issue with the force of a linebacker.

What does a controlling woman look like? If you think she looks like a drill sergeant with a whip, think again. Sometimes she looks like an angel with a spatula, light pink lip gloss, and sweet words laced with sour intent. Consider these characteristics of a controlling woman:

- won't let anyone help in the kitchen or around the house but complains that if *she* doesn't do the chores, they won't be done right
- uses nagging as a tool because if she doesn't "remind" her kids, husband, or coworkers to do certain things, they will never budge
- claims she wants a strong husband who leads but shatters him with her words, criticism, or silence when he tries to
- continues to do things like waking up her older kids in the morning instead of asking them to set an alarm because she knows if she doesn't awaken them, they will sleep through class (my son tells me about a mom who still calls her college-aged son to wake him up daily)

Though I never viewed control as one of my stark issues, I've come to realize that my controlling nature is just snuggled in a cozier blanket than the ones others own. My words are sweeter but can still pack a punch. Donald Miller, author of *Blue like Jazz*, once stated that the opposite of love is not hate but control.

I'll never forget the day I faced the dragon of control like a princess with a toothpick for a weapon. Our infant son was strapped in the back seat of our minivan as I pulled up to the elementary school to pick up our first grade daughter, Brooke, and our kindergarten lamb, Ally. Brooke was always social, flitting here and there with a lot of playdates and invites. But Ally was different. She was shy and timid. When Ally was in preschool, Bobby and I had a half-hour ritual just to drop her off for an hour-and-a-half class.

This was a big day for Ally, as she had finally felt comfortable enough to invite a friend over to play. They came tumbling out of the school and spotted me waving like crazy from our van. Brooke piled in first, then Ally and her little buddy, along with the two kids we took turns carpooling with. Little Suzanne from the carpool crew was famous for being bossy, so it wasn't surprising to hear her bark out a command: "Come over to *my* house! I don't have anyone to play with. Or ... hey, can I play with you guys?"

Without even a consulting glance at Ally, I invited bossy Suzanne to join Ally and her buddy for the afternoon. No amount of brownies or Kool-Aid could salvage that playdate. After the lambs left our home and Ally and I had a moment together sitting on the wooden stairs of our home, I asked her if she had a good time. "It wasn't really that fun, Mommy," she sighed. She didn't cry, but suddenly I began to sob like a dam had been breached. As I tried to gain composure so I could explain to my five-year-old what I was feeling, I uttered an apology that welled up from the deepest place in my soul. "Sweetie, Mommy needs to ask you to forgive me. I had no right to invite someone else to your special time with your friend. I was just trying to make everyone happy, and instead I made *you* unhappy." With curled fingers and puckered lips Ally kissed the tears on my face and told me it was OK, but I have never forgotten this lesson — that sometimes good women who try to control everyone's happiness and moods end up the unhappiest of all.

Control is the ultimate counterfeit of love. It's the secret adulteress to good intent. Like a robber who has been hiding in a dark closet, control ambushes us. It gags us and then surveys what it can take from our lives without our ever realizing what has happened.

At times I wonder if I'll ever stop having to pull the gag off my mouth. Will my longings and my need to control shift from a roar to a quiet whimper? I have wrestled with this question for years and fleshed out my thinking in the safe retreat of countless notebook pages on which my mental meanderings are visible only to God. It's here that I've rehearsed the longings we all crave: a longing to be nurtured; a longing for intimacy, purpose, and discipline; and — the pinnacle of all longing — the longing to be treasured.

Curled up around these longings lay a brood of substitutes. The substitutes replace the true longings. Nurture turns to control. Intimacy pushes back as distrust. Purpose cools to bland insecurity. Discipline slows to laziness. And being treasured changes into being trampled or ignored.

Looking at my worn journal pages stained with tears of frustration that show how I have tried to cope through counterfeit substitutes, a thought dawns on me like the glow of a sunrise: Longings that languish in the "self mode" typically end in fear and control, while longings that bend toward God turn to faith.

When we determine to understand our Spirit hunger, to hold out so that our real longings are filled by a real God, our lives will look different. We move from having an insatiable need for control to a desperate need for faith.

chapter 3

—

WANDERING, WONDERING, AND FLAKES

I've often been asked if the life of a professional athlete is a glamorous one. Although it does have its moments, the tidbit I like to readily share is that we moved *forty-seven times* in a ten-year time span. That's right, forty-seven times! We only counted it a move if we had to establish electric and phone service — so there were a few more moves that didn't make the count. After being unexpectedly released by the Texas Rangers one spring training, we got the call from our agent that we needed to be in Los Angeles in forty-eight hours. He was working on a new deal with a team and wanted us to be close to him. Because spring training camp was in the southern tip of Florida, this presented a real problem. I will never forget my husband and I stuffing things into our van, literally leaving the cribs for our daughters, ages two and three, on the curb for the apartment manager because we couldn't strap them to the roof of our van!

I was struggling with serious morning (and afternoon and evening) sickness from my third pregnancy with our son, and I rocked slowly in the front seat, toothbrush in hand, counting the hours until we arrived in Los Angeles. We hadn't even been in California for one hour before our agent called and said, "Good news! You're going to sign with the Pittsburgh Pirates and play minor-league ball in Buffalo, New York."

Bobby got on a plane the next morning as I crawled into a bed at his parents' home in Orange County and regrouped for a few days before meeting him as he joined yet another new team. Glamour indeed!

During this time our oldest daughter sucked on a pacifier like her life depended on it. I tried to break her of the habit, but she seemed to have mini-convulsions that scared the living daylights out of us all. One day, I asked her pediatrician if it was abnormal for a three-and-a-half-year-old to still suck a binky. Knowing the kind of lifestyle we led, he asked a profound question: "How many different beds has she slept in during the last six months?" As I began counting, he calmly interrupted and said, "When you go to bed at night, you have your husband beside you. If she needs the pacifier to comfort her through all your moves, let her have it. But when the time is right, you will need to replace it with a different type of comfort that she will be mature enough to cling to."

I never thought a little rubber nipple in a plastic ring could teach me such valuable life lessons, but it did. If a pacifier's role is to comfort, soothe, and diminish crying and fussing, I began to think about the adult binkies we tend to reach for. Food, alcohol, sex, clothing, mirrors, crazy-full schedules, control — anything to numb or divert us.

Is it wrong to enjoy a few cookies? Of course not, but how about a dozen?

Is it wrong to buy a few things for yourself or for the house? Certainly not. But what about when your credit cards are maxed out and you really can't afford to spend any more money?

Is it wrong to enjoy a glass of wine? What happens, though, when just thinking about it is the only thing that gets you through the day?

Is it wrong to want things done just right? To have your kids and spouse meet high standards of excellence? Nothing wrong with excellence, but what about when your standards become crushing and no one can do enough to really please you?

Enjoying pleasures in life is perfectly normal. As a matter of fact, God intends us to find pleasure in life. But anything that nudges us toward secrecy, anxiety, or shame stems from Satan's lie that we can feed our own appetites. They become a substitute for Spirit hunger when they escalate into a type of compulsivity. When the need becomes greater than the pleasure, we've moved into chaos. We can numb and stuff ourselves in a myriad of ways, but Spirit hunger is filled by God himself — not by Satan's cunning substitutes.

Wandering and Wondering

We live in what I call a modern-day slave market. Sometimes we are lined up against our will on a slave block, watched by guilty eyes that relish the sight of helpless men and women about to meet with destruction. And sometimes we climb onto that block by ourselves, chains clanking and dragging behind us as we gaze out over the crowd, wondering if anyone notices our bondage. Being a former chain carrier myself, my spirit bows in gratitude to the One who unravels chains one link at a time.

A story of chains in the book of Exodus is so powerful it practically takes away my breath. The Israelites, the apple of God's eye, were slaves in a cruel Egyptian regime that stubbornly kept them captive and oppressed for generations. I've often thought the Israelites were bizarrely lucky, because as bad as their slavery was, at least they knew who to be mad at! They could rally against the Egyptians in the privacy of their homes, in the conversations among the Hebrew leaders, and in the pillow talk between husband and wife. They clearly knew who to spew at.

But all that changed when they proudly marched behind Moses out of Egypt in a reverie of disbelief and awe. "Can this be happening? Are we really leaving the land that has so cruelly raped our heritage?" They celebrated and worshiped as they participated in the most spectacular exodus ever recorded in mankind's history.

But after a mere two months of freedom, the grumblings and complaining began. Two months is not a long time. Think June and July of the summer. That's no time at all when you compare it to generations of abuse and prejudice. So after this tiny trickle of days, the whole crowd is ready to rumble:

> In the desert the whole community grumbled against Moses and Aaron. The Israelites said to them, "If only we had died by the LORD's hand in Egypt! There we sat around pots of meat and ate all the food we wanted, but you have brought us out into this desert to starve this entire assembly to death."
>
> Exodus 16:2 – 3

Two months was all it took for this group to choose bread and meat over freedom and glory. Sometimes I think that if we had ears to hear the sighs of heaven, they might blow us right off the planet. I once heard a man joke about someone he knew who lived a miserable lifestyle. When confronted about his choices, he stammered, "I may live in hell, but at least I know all the street names!"

These verses from Exodus are pregnant with meaning as we face the fact that sometimes God brings us to new, exciting places — but we're prone to complaining and compulsion. Moses goes to God in prayer for this murmuring crowd, and God lays out his plan:

> Then the LORD said to Moses, "I will rain down bread from heaven for you. The people are to go out each day and gather enough for that day. In this way I will test them and see whether they will follow my instructions."
>
> Exodus 16:4

God was very clear in this mandate. The people had a role in his provision, and he had a role in it too. God's role was to rain down bread from heaven. This was revolutionary because up until that point, bread was only shaped and baked by women's hands. Raining from heaven was off the script — but so was walking through the sea — a now distant memory when it came to trusting God.

The people's role in this mandate was precise. They were to follow God's instructions. He rains; they walk. He provides; they believe he will.

What happens next is so stunning that it's almost funny. God continues to unravel the way his people have framed his personality.

> "I have heard the grumblings of the sons of Israel; speak to them, saying, 'At twilight you shall eat meat, and in the morning you shall be filled with bread; and you shall know that I am the LORD your God.'"
>
> So it came about at evening that the quails came up and covered the camp, and in the morning there was a layer of dew around the camp.
>
> When the layer of dew evaporated, behold, on the surface of the wilderness there was a fine *flake-like thing*, fine as the frost on the ground.
>
> When the sons of Israel saw it, they said to one another, "What is it?" For they did not know what it was. And Moses said to them, "It is the bread which the LORD has given you to eat."
>
> Exodus 16:12 – 15 NASB, emphasis mine

Quails wandering around camp at night—that's self-explanatory. The Israelites knew this was their meat, but the bread was a bit confusing. When they saw the ground covered by a "flake-like thing," they were perplexed. "What is it?" they asked with scrunched faces and squinting eyes. Moses explained the provision with confidence and grace: "This is the bread God promised." I can see their faces, hands scratching heads as they whispered, "Sure doesn't look like bread to me."

The weight of this event is profound. They didn't recognize the bread because it didn't come in the form they thought it would be. It wasn't baked yet, but it was provided. I'm reminded of how often in my life I've walked right past the flake-like thing, expecting a golden loaf that's ready to slice.

About fifteen years ago, I was asked to be a speaker at a conference for pro athletes' wives. I was a breakout session speaker, and the keynote speaker was a woman named Beth Moore. One night after a session, Beth and I huddled arm in arm talking to one another. I told her it was my life's passion to write books and speak, a path on which she was picking up traction. At that time, God had me teaching elementary school because we were struggling financially to make ends meet. And I was raising our three children mostly by myself because of Bobby's job in the minor leagues. We prayed for each other and for the trajectory God would take in laying out the plans he had for our lives. Her path catapulted her to international recognition as someone who was changing the face of women's ministry in this country, while my path led to runny noses and parent-teacher conferences.

"Where's my bread?" I asked at times, wondering if I had wasted the last decade and a half of my life. What I failed to realize was that through each year and circumstance, God was uniquely equipping me for a life of writing and speaking that would go beyond my wildest dreams. My skill set grew its own set of wings, holding me in place until I was ready to fly.

Are we walking by our flakes, thinking that what is covering the surface of our lives is a detour from the real plan? May I gently propose that the flake *is* the plan? It's exactly what God was trying to teach his people: "I provide. And even though it may not come in the form you expect, I will teach you to bake it and enjoy it. *It will be exactly what you need.*"

MAGGOTS AND MOANS

Once God's people got over the fact that their bread was provided in an unexpected way, things got really interesting. Moses told the masses that they should gather the manna according to the number of people in their tents. He also instructed them to use a unit of measurement called an omer, which is equivalent to approximately 3 pounds. It's quite a picture to imagine more than a million people gathering flakes with a scooper, accumulating their omers. But they did as they were told ... well, almost.

> Then Moses said to them, "No one is to keep any of it until morning."
> However, some of them paid no attention to Moses; they kept part of it until morning, but it was full of maggots and began to smell. So Moses was angry with them.
>
> Exodus 16:19 – 20

Right here in these verses, we see the first control freaks with food. The first gluttons on record. Although they were instructed to gather only what they needed each day, some felt the need to sneak it into their tents. To stuff it away for later. To save it for a rainy day.

Maybe God is holding out on us.

Maybe he won't really show up.

Certainly it won't hurt for us to take this matter into our own hands.

And the whispered lies from the garden continue to spew.

These first gluttons quickly learned that what we try to store away as counterfeit stuffing eventually breeds worms. God wasn't holding back his provision for his beloved, he was showering it on them. Inviting his own into a daily communion of trust capable of shattering their frightened disposition to hoard.

I've learned my greatest life lessons from food. There is not one kind of behavior regarding food that I haven't pitifully participated in. Bingeing, purging, starving, overeating, sneaking, managing — you name it, I've done it. One day in college, as I sat in my apartment mate's empty room, I gazed at a picture of Jesus on the wall. He is handsomely looking out into the distance, hair blowing in the wind, with a smile that was able to trace the fractured imprint of my soul.

I was trying to think of a painless way to take my life, because frankly, I saw no way out of the nightmare I was living when it came to food. Compulsion was raging wildly as I began to put weight on my body that had withered away through my obsession with control. My entire face had broken out with acne, which I later learned was the result of malnutrition. But I was dating a baseball star, for goodness' sake — cake on some makeup and act like everything's fine.

On this day, I knew that nothing was fine. I was done, and my life needed to end. I looked up at the picture stunningly staring back at me, and I heaved a cry so desperate it shattered the silence. "If you are real, Jesus, whoever you are, please make yourself known to me. You're the last thing I'll try."

No earthquake could match the way my life shook that day. I dug out an old Bible that I had never opened, and the words seemed to leap off the pages. No religion, no one pushing ideology on me — just a real healing and transformation so true that I, thankfully, was never the same.

Ironically, my first book was born from this healing and from the freedom I eventually enjoyed. I titled it *Truly Fed*, and every time I rub my hand across its smooth cover, I'm reminded of the flakes God used in my life to bake manna.

From hoarder to one who trusts. From worm breeder to one who believes. This is the way of those who refuse the counterfeit and learn to let their baskets of omers be filled daily.

chapter 4

—

SACRED MAKEOVERS

*N*othing comforts me more than knowing that Jesus completely
understands how hard it is to walk around in these bodies, fighting our "head noise" with valiant attempts toward a faith we can believe
in but can't see. A brilliant Scripture spills this promise right over our
lives: "Because [Jesus] himself suffered when he was tempted, he is able
to help those who are being tempted" (Hebrews 2:18).

To think that the Son of God rallied against the lies and whispers
that tried to numb him to his Father is strangely comforting. He never
asks us to do something he wasn't willing to do.

At Jesus' baptism, he emerged from the currents of the Jordan River
to be greeted by the sound of his Father's voice proclaiming, "This is My
beloved Son, in whom I am well-pleased" (Matthew 3:17 NASB). And
Jesus does something completely unpredictable. Instead of basking in
this moment of glory, he heads to the wilderness to be tempted by the
devil. After forty long days of prayer and fasting, he is hungry. He is ripe
and ready for a showdown with lies. The tempter comes as expected
and delicately pounces on Jesus' physical weakness:

> The tempter came to him and said, "If you are the Son of God, tell these stones to become bread."
>
> Jesus answered, "It is written: 'Man shall not live on bread alone, but on every word that comes from the mouth of God.'"
>
> Matthew 4:3 – 4

Satan knew well and good that Jesus was the Son of God, but he was trying to make Jesus question this truth. It is no accident that the first temptation was launched from hunger. We still seem to get our physical appetites and hunger mixed up with our Spirit hunger. Substituting and controlling suffice for the real hunger that wells up within us. But Jesus won't have any part of it. He confronts Satan with the force of a debate champion, quoting Scripture right back into his hideous face.

I wonder what our lives might look like if instead of numbing or stuffing, we simply were to state, "It is written." Jesus knew this was the right battle plan, and it is still the most effective tool we have today.

Interestingly, the Scripture he used to shoot down this lie takes us right back to the flake-like thing that was lying on the ground for the Israelites:

> He humbled you and let you be hungry, and fed you with manna which you did not know, nor did your fathers know, that He might make you understand that man does not live by bread alone, but man lives by everything that proceeds out of the mouth of the Lord.
>
> Deuteronomy 8:3 NASB

The potent truth is that God lets us be hungry, spiritually and physically, so he can fill us with manna that we did not know. His food changes the whole landscape. The question is this: Can we discard our pacifiers for a deeper Spirit hunger that longs to be fed?

I lived in a food coma for nearly eight years. I based my moods, outlook, and self-worth on the number I saw on a scale. Like a hospital patient hooked up to tubes and machines, I was surviving but not thriving. Breathing but not living.

After an initial blast of healing in college the day I asked Jesus if he was real, I devoured the Bible like a kid eats pudding. I savored its taste and texture as I watched it literally restore my broken mind to sanity. But I still struggled with lingering thoughts and behaviors that wrestled me into a state of self-hatred.

As I stood in front of my closet one day, beating myself up over clothes I couldn't zip or over the fat rolls I pictured bulging from my clothes, I knew I had to transact business with God or I would drown in an insecure pool of hypocrisy.

I'll never forget strapping my fourteen-month-old daughter, Brooke, and newborn, Ally, into the car and heading for the nearest bookstore. I was crying so loudly you could have heard me in the houses lining the wooded highway I was driving down.

The God I love says I can have life and have it abundantly. This is not abundance; it's prison. If the truth sets us free, I've got to get some truth.

Here I was, wife of the shortstop for the New York Yankees and Bible study leader to the wives on our team, speeding down the highway to get me some truth. And boy, did I find some. In a quest to finally toss my favorite pacifier into the trash, I found truth.

I studied. I prayed. I read. I confessed. I went after freedom like a prisoner who sees a jail cell key slowly snaking its way under the cell door. A true Spirit filling was what I wanted, not more Band-Aids and ointment. The problem with counterfeit fillings is that they keep us numb to a greater filling.

What Are We Yoked To?

As an avid observer of people and gender traits, I've found that men and women handle their pain differently. Men tend to turn outward with their pain, while women turn inward. This explains why many more men struggle with pornography or infidelity than women. As women, we'd rather hurt *ourselves*. I would walk on a bed of rusty nails before I'd look at a pornographic image. I'm not ranking sin or deceit, as if some types are worse than others; it's just that sexual sin does nothing for me. But I'll beat myself up with damaging thoughts, poor self-image, food comfort, bitterness, or gossip — *now* we're talking.

In the gospel of Matthew, Jesus is speaking to the multitudes when he offers an invitation laced with a hope so deep that you can almost experience a spiritual massage just by reading it:

> "Come to me, all you who are weary and burdened, and I will give you rest. Take my yoke upon you and learn from me, for I am gentle and humble in heart, and you will find rest for your souls. For my yoke is easy and my burden is light."
>
> Matthew 11:28 – 30

Jesus cleverly joined together the most unlikely mix of words. Words that don't fit at all in their scope of purpose: *weary, burdened, rest, yoke, gentle, humble, burden, light*. Although we don't often talk about yokes today, when Jesus walked this earth, a yoke was a symbol that people would recognize. Yokes were wooden frames that harnessed together two animals for the purpose of pulling. People also wore yokes as a frame designed to fit across their shoulders with balanced loads at each end.

When Jesus gives the stunning invitation to take *his yoke* upon us, to strap it across our shoulders so we are pulling with him, all of a sudden the harsh view of a wooden apparatus with splinters looks inviting. Jesus then says that once we are strapped together, we will learn from him and get to explore the gentle, humble ways of his heart, which led him to the cross. As if that's not enough, he promises rest for our souls and a load that is light.

Why in the world do we yoke ourselves to things that aren't good? That aren't gentle or humble or light or restful. That aren't Jesus?

Paul clearly understood this plight when he wrote, "It is for freedom that Christ has set us free. Stand firm, then, and do not let yourselves be burdened again by a yoke of slavery" (Galatians 5:1). It's interesting that the ones who subject us to a yoke of slavery are *ourselves*. Plain and simple, we choose our yokes.

The weight of this verdict sends me right back to my crumpled journal pages. I realize I need to settle into the truth and discover what's going on in my life. If Jesus wrote a blurb to describe his yoke, these are the words he would use to describe it: *gentle, humble, restful, light.* Truthfully, my own blurb would sound like this: *anxiety, fear, tired, a heaviness that screams, "I'll never be enough."*

Jesus' yoke beckons like a warm bath. We step in and find soothing comfort for our aching lives. My yoke screams like a cold shower that never ends. Icy water drenching goose-bumped skin, desperate for a warm towel to wrap myself in.

FROM YOKE TO STRONGHOLD

The problem with yokes is that what I attach myself to can silently morph into a stronghold if left unchecked. A stronghold is like a yoke that has grown from toddler to teenager. It calls the shots and thinks it knows everything. Habits, alliances, and behaviors that sit right under the surface of our lives, swelling with a rancid stench — these are the strongholds that numb us to a greater Spirit filling.

Ironically, the original domain for the word *stronghold* belonged to God, until Satan bullied the word onto his court. Consider these words of David:

> The LORD also will be a *stronghold* for the oppressed,
> A *stronghold* in times of trouble.
>
> Psalm 9:9 NASB, emphasis mine

> But as for me, I shall sing of Your strength;
> Yes, I shall joyfully sing of Your lovingkindness in the morning,
> For You have been my *stronghold*

And a refuge in the day of my distress.
O my strength, I will sing praises to You;
For God is my *stronghold*, the God who shows me lovingkindness.

Psalm 59:16–17 NASB, emphasis mine

David knew what it was like to run from trouble. From people who wanted to hurt him and family members who thought he was a self-centered loser. But he also knew where he needed to go for protection — straight into the stronghold of God.

Defined as a defensible place, a place that is fortified and easily protected, you can just hear the authority of God breathing down on trouble like a bull ready to enter the ring. It's as if he's shouting, "Come to me. Stay with me. Don't mess with that. Don't believe that. My arms are encircling you, and they are strong enough to hold you in my hiding place."

My husband, Bobby, and I know a thing or two about strongholds. Both the kind that push us into the fort of God and the kind that kick us out.

Right around our ten-year wedding anniversary, I began to sense something wasn't right. After spending five years in the majors with the New York Yankees, we were bouncing around the minor leagues trying to recapture a major-league position. Although we usually tried to keep our family together (remember the forty-seven moves?), there was a season of time when my doctor wouldn't let me travel at the end of a risky pregnancy. Bobby was in the throes of a difficult situation with his career — undervalued, discarded, no longer a star. In the midst of this pain, an idea surfaced one lonely night as he walked the floor of his hotel room. "I'll just go down to the hotel bar and see what happens."

Down the stairs he descended. The chapel leader of every team he ever played on, loving father and husband, son of two proud parents — he crept to the hotel bar to "see what happens." Wedding ring absent, he enters the bar as if walking into a foreign land. A land he hadn't had a passport to until now. An unattractive woman seemed to take a liking to him, and suddenly, repulsed by her attention, he removed himself from that foreign place, panting as he reached his room, grabbing the Bible that had been his compass for years.

When Bobby bravely shared this story with me years later, we were already in triage, trying to resuscitate our shattered marriage. The night in the lonely hotel room, wedding ring left sitting on a bedside table, was the beginning of a stronghold so belligerent that it took our marriage hostage. Secrets, lies, unholy trysts that whisper comfort but bring death — this was the land Bobby lived in until he boldly crawled to a different stronghold.

During a four-month separation, he sought God's face like never before. He filled notebooks with the truths God spoke over his life as he wept in utter disbelief at the grace held out to him. We cried, moaned, screamed, and loved. Through dark months that held the delicate promise of the dawn of a new day, we sought truth and restoration as if our lives depended on it. And truthfully, they did. God's "defensible place" is now Bobby's home where no foreign entity is invited in or allowed to invade.

A Place for Rebuilding

How do we recognize when a harmless pattern we're mildly attached to is sliding into something that is furiously attached to *us*? When an innocent yoke changes into a strangling stronghold? And more important, what do we do when we realize it's choking us?

A fascinating story about strongholds is buried in the book of Judges, with its hero being an unlikely man named Gideon. When we first meet Gideon, he is beating the daylights out of wheat in a winepress in order to keep it from the menacing Midianites. For seven years the people of Israel would sow their crops, only to have them pillaged at harvest time by the Midianites and Amalekites. This continued year after year, and the situation became so bad that many of the Israelites had run for the hills, living in caves and dens.

One day, as Gideon was trying to protect his family's wheat, an angel of the Lord came to him and said, "The LORD is with you, O valiant warrior" (Judges 6:12 NASB). I love how God nicknames us long before we match his description. Gideon was feeling like anything but a valiant warrior. As a matter of fact, he had an attitude problem to go along with a poor self-image.

> "Pardon me, my lord," Gideon replied, "but if the LORD is with us, why has all this happened to us? Where are all his wonders that our ancestors told us about when they said, 'Did not the LORD bring us up out of Egypt?' But now the LORD has abandoned us and given us into the hand of Midian."
>
> Judges 6:13

Instead of being honored that he was speaking to an angel, Gideon brazenly reminds the angel that he has heard the stories about this God who does miracles, but he isn't impressed with his recent résumé. He simply states, "God has abandoned us."

The great thing about God is that he can handle the gut punches we throw at him. Gideon was punching, but God delivered the knockout blow. He looks at Gideon and tells him that *he* is the one chosen to deliver Israel from the Midianites.

Immediately Gideon has an insecure response as he whines, "My family is the least important within our tribe, Manasseh, and I'm the youngest in my father's house." Surprisingly, God doesn't care what self-doubt plagues us. He looks for people willing to say a gutsy yes to him, regardless of how impossible a task may seem.

Later that night God stretched Gideon even further with a task that scared the wheat out of him.

> Now on the same night the LORD said to him, "Take your father's bull and a second bull seven years old, and pull down the altar of Baal which belongs to your father, and cut down the Asherah [a wooden symbol of female deity] that is beside it; and build an altar to the LORD your God *on the top of this stronghold* in an orderly

manner, and take a second bull and offer a burnt offering with the wood of the Asherah which you shall cut down."

Judges 6:25 – 26 NASB, emphasis mine

Not only was God commissioning Gideon for daunting service; he was asking him to clean up his father's backyard from strongholds that were an affront to him. The part of this passage that stuns and thrills me is that God asks him to tear down the stronghold — fake and insulting — and build an altar to him right on top of the heinous counterfeit. Right on top of it!

We're often blind to the things that are sprouting and thriving in our backyards. Bitterness over a past wound we won't let go of, habits we secretly feed, jealousy we nurse and absorb. We curse the very image we are made in as we stand before a mirrored reflection.

God asks us to first tear it down. To recognize the stronghold and scratch and claw at its structure in our lives until it's a pile of rubble. Then he outrageously asks us to build an altar to him right on top of the former destruction.

THE PROCESS OF A MAKEOVER

Recognize: What is numbing me to a greater filling from God? What yokes have I attached myself to that are now strongholds in my life?

Renounce: Once identified, we begin to tear down the former stronghold with the power of prayer, God's Word, confession, and resolve.

Rebuild: Using the wood of former idols, we rebuild this area with the assurance that God never wastes a moment in our lives. Even those moments we would rather run from, God uses for brilliant transformation. This may take the form, eventually, of sharing past struggles with a fellow traveler, encouraging them as one who has walked before them, or teaching our children a different way of dealing with the temptations of this world.

Like Gideon, we are called to smash our idols, go after the strongholds, throw away our binkies, and rebuild right on top of former destruction. The reason God asks us to do this isn't to torture us or take away from us the things we like; it's to prepare us for a greater filling. A filling that our Spirit hunger moans for and craves. A Spirit hunger that fully engages God.

PART TWO

a heart that seeks

chapter 5

—

ENGAGING GOD …
HOW DO WE PRAY?

*M*y grandmother was a living contradiction. A banker's wife who one day could hold a fistful of cards while playing bridge, nails painted a perfect shade of red. The next day a daredevil woman sitting at the wheel of a red Jeep, hurtling us up the steep edge of a Colorado mountain at high speeds. I once remember her saying, "Honey, sometimes you have to drive through a lot of muck to get to the good hills."

So it is with our pursuit of Spirit hunger. We've had to drive through the muck of counterfeit and numbing to get to the good stuff, but now here we are, ready to plunge into the spacious meadows of engaging God.

The easiest way we engage God is prayer, but prayer is anything but easy. Richard Foster writes, "Real prayer comes not from gritting our teeth but from falling in love."[3] I know I'm in love with God, but why do I often feel like I'm left gritting my teeth? Foster shares a story that sheds light on how prayer can get beyond the grinding stage and into a friendlier time with God.

One day a friend of mine was walking through a shopping mall with his two-year-old son. The child was in a particularly cantankerous mood, fussing and fuming. The frustrated father tried everything to quiet his son, but nothing seemed to help. The child simply would not obey. Then, under some special inspiration, the father scooped up his son and, holding him close to his chest, began singing an impromptu love song. None of the words rhymed. He sang off key. And yet, as best as he could, this father began sharing his heart. "I love you," he sang. "I'm so glad you're my boy. You make me happy. I like the way you laugh." On they went from one store to the next. Quietly the father continued singing off key and making up words that did not rhyme. The child relaxed and became still, listening to this strange and wonderful song. Finally, they finished shopping and went to the car. As the father opened the door and prepared to buckle his son into the car seat, the child lifted his head and said simply, "Sing it to me again, Daddy! Sing it to me again!"[4]

This is a priceless picture of a daddy who holds us when we're in the throes of a teeth-grinding fit. A two-way blessing occurs in which Daddy feels loved and child feels embraced.

WHY DO WE STRUGGLE IN PRAYER?

This type of connection is something we long to wrap ourselves in, yet many women confide in me that although they've experienced times of power and movement in prayer, they find it hard to stay connected over time. In my ponderings I've found a few reasons I think we struggle: we've fallen victim to praying with formulas; our prayers have become repetitive and stale; and finally, we lack stamina or staying power when we pray.

Formulaic Praying

The sad fact that something as exciting as communicating with God could be stuffed into a formula is a tale as old as time. We are prone to formulas because they guarantee results (or at least they seem to).

After many years of teaching elementary school and a career as a national consultant for the Public Education and Business Coalition, I have the hindsight to see a sad trend. When the push for test performance swept across our country, districts and classroom teachers went into panic mode. "What are we doing wrong?" "Why aren't our kids performing on these tests?" Slowly, real novels were replaced with scripted reading programs "guaranteed" to raise test scores. Entire districts adopted reading plans that often pushed real reading off the schedule, replacing it with computer-driven tests and worksheets with bubbled-in responses. Allegiance to programs *about* reading replaced *authentic* reading.

This is where many women find themselves when it comes to prayer. After reading popular books designed to help us pray, we still feel insecure if a scripted prayer isn't written out at the end of a chapter. The formula may feel helpful at first, but like a person who follows countless diets on a quest to lose weight, once the diet is over, the same behavior reigns. There's no real growth in our engagement of God.

When my daughters were in high school, I attended a prayer meeting that was part of a national movement of mothers praying for their school-age children. Being a lover of prayer, I couldn't wait to meet these ladies and deeply touch God's heart for our high school kids. After two meetings I never went back. The first time I showed up, the leader had a card in her hand that she followed like a surgery schedule in a hospital. One woman was mid-sentence in her tearful prayer request when she was cut off by the leader. "Time for the next part of our meeting," she chirped. "We need to move on to a quick Scripture reading." I truly don't think the Holy Spirit himself could have budged this woman off her schedule. I looked around at the other women and wondered if they were as squelched as I was. Sadly, they seemed to be used to this type of gathering. I walked away, realizing that allegiance to a structure rather than to the overflow of our spirit's need to connect to God is stifling.

Repetitive and Stale Praying

Another reason we tend to struggle with prayer is that it becomes repetitive and stale. There's certainly nothing wrong with reciting beautiful prayers much loved through the ages, like the Lord's Prayer. They offer comfort and a corporate unity that surely connects believers' souls. But to never move beyond the recited prayers of our youth is a little like surviving on appetizers rather than enjoying a full meal. In the gospel of Matthew, Jesus makes a bold statement about prayer: "And when you are praying, do not use meaningless repetition as the Gentiles do, for they suppose that they will be heard for their many words" (Matthew 6:7 NASB).

The problem with meaningless repetition is that it offers no engagement with the Father. Reciting the same things over and over with no heart connection is a little like saying, "Scooby-Dooby-Doo, where are you? Scooby-Dooby-Doo, where are you?" It's cartoon gibberish in the language of God.

My sister and I sat at my son's high school football game one cold Friday night, and to take my worried mind off the fact that every time he caught a pass he was being demolished by guys twice his size, we started to recite some of the prayers we were taught to repeatedly say in our youth. I giggled as I shouted, "Remember the one called 'the act of contrition'?" This is a beautifully written prayer that shares the pangs of sorrow we feel for sins we commit. I shouted above the crowd that I could never understand why someone would write a prayer that starts out by saying, "O my God, I am hardly sorry for having offended Thee." She looked at me, mystified, and said, "Gar, that's not what it says. It says, 'I'm *heartily* sorry for having offended Thee!'" Oops! I probably said that prayer a thousand times in my youth and never even knew what I was saying!

Repetition will never get us a better audience with God. As a matter of fact, it's a bit like living by a busy highway — constant noise settling over the backdrop of real conversation. This repetition is not to be confused with praying for the same things over and over. That's persistence — which is a plus in God's column. We're talking about droning on and on with words that cycle in our heads and out of our mouths, with no meaning or relevance attached.

Lack of Stamina or Staying Power in Our Prayers

Every new school year, I would gather wide-eyed third graders around an anchor chart where we prepared to create a class poster titled "Our Class Stamina." We defined it as "the ability to stick with something." To be able to focus uninterrupted on things that were important to us. We added to the chart things that help build our stamina, as well as things that drain it. I still refer to the wisdom of third graders when I engage God in prayer, because without stamina, we stay stuck in a fluster of mindless distractions and rabbit trails.

How can I be begging God for healing in a person's life and suddenly be thinking about my grocery list? On my knees crying out for insight into a situation and mentally float toward what I want to watch on TV that night? It's maddening but true; our fickle minds need some focus. I've learned to keep a small pad of sticky notes near me when I'm praying. When a distracting thought pops up, I simply take it out of my brain and put it on the sticky note. If I try to stuff the thought away, it seems to grow, choking out my spirit's dining with God. So sticky notes in hand, I rope my mind into a focused frenzy and pray.

It's comforting to know we aren't the only ones who have a bit of Attention Deficit Disorder when it comes to prayer. Jesus' closest friends — Peter, James, and John — struggled with this continually. Distraction and drowsiness seemed to derail their praying, much like they do ours today.

About eight days after Jesus fed five thousand people, he took his three friends up onto a mountain to pray. While Jesus was praying, his appearance changed, and his clothes became white and gleaming. Supernatural things were happening on that mountain as Moses and Elijah spoke to Jesus about his imminent death in Jerusalem. You would think James, John, and Peter would be sitting on the edge of their seats, prayerfully and reverently absorbing the weight of this experience. But this is not what happened.

> Peter and his companions were very sleepy, but when they became fully awake, they saw his glory and the two men standing with him.
>
> Luke 9:32

"Very sleepy"? For the love of Pete, how is it possible to be nodding off when you're on a mountain with a Savior who is transforming before your eyes? I've often wondered if this feeling of drowsiness just bowled them over, or if after waiting for some action over the course of several hours they just got bored and their eyes got heavy. Either way, it's a bit perplexing. To make matters worse, this drowsiness and distraction happened again, but this time with much more at stake:

> They went to a place called Gethsemane, and Jesus said to his disciples, "Sit here while I pray." He took Peter, James and John along with him, and he began to be deeply distressed and troubled. "My soul is overwhelmed with sorrow to the point of death," he said to them. "Stay here and keep watch."
>
> Then he returned to his disciples and found them sleeping. "Simon," he said to Peter, "are you asleep? Couldn't you keep watch for one hour? Watch and pray so that you will not fall into temptation. *The spirit is willing, but the flesh is weak.*"
>
> Mark 14:32 – 34, 37 – 38, emphasis mine

Embedded in this tearful conversation, Creator speaking to the created, Jesus explains the tug-of-war we engage in today. The spirit is willing, but the flesh is weak. As much as we want to pray, plan to stay awake, or desire to please God by lifting up others, our flesh struggles to keep up with our spirit's intent. I've often wondered if these men fell asleep because it was too much to humanly experience these depths of God.

How would you ever unravel the sight of Jesus heaving before his Father in fear? Or make sense of a gleaming Savior speaking to prophets revered since childhood? Author Tricia McCary Rhodes refers to what Teresa of Avila called a "holy drowsiness." Rhodes writes, "Many people feel guilty when prayer lulls them to sleep. Some ancient contemplatives felt this to be a special place in the heart of God. Francis of Sales said, 'I had rather be asleep on the breast of God than awake in any other place.'"[5]

Perhaps God in his ultimate wisdom and grace gently lets us sleep when he knows our minds can only take so much of his glory.

THE LURE OF WORRY

Jesus has much to say about prayer. Engaging God in this way is something he begs us to do. So with the determination of an ant carrying a log, I am committed to seeking to understand this engagement fully.

I've discovered that often what I think is prayer is really worry with a few God words at the beginning and end: "Dear Father, worry, worry, worry, worry ... In Jesus' name. Amen."

While distraction leads us away from prayer, worry cozies us up next to it, but what we often practice as prayer is a sliver of faith wrapped in a blanket of panic. Worry restates negative trust in fearful outcomes. It is the belief that what you dread will be the outcome of what you pray.

What if my husband [or boyfriend] leaves me or is unfaithful?
What if my kids get hurt in an accident?
What if I fail at my job?
What if I never get healthy or feel well?
What if we go under financially?

The "what ifs" create drama in our heads so intense that Hollywood would be put to shame.

When I was raising teenagers, my friends and I would joke that we could have our teens from the front door to the grave in about fourteen seconds. As they would leave for school each morning or for a night out with friends, I would shout, "Jesus loves you! Make good choices!"

Essentially, I was saying, "If you get hurt or anything happens to you, I don't know if I can bear it — so be really smart and careful, or I'll kill you!" I spent many a night "worry praying" my way through the hours until my kids were safely back in their beds, sensing that worry is like a rocking chair — it consumes a lot of energy and takes you nowhere.

Oswald Chambers wrote, "It is not only wrong to worry, it is infidelity, because worrying means that we do not think that God can look after the practical details of our lives, and it is never anything else that worries us."[6] Why are we apt to cheat on God before we trust him? Why does trust feel risky and worry feel natural? I've spent a lot of hours pursuing answers to these "worry" questions, and I've come to realize that *authentic prayer* lasers its focus on the goodness of God, while worry teases the imagination to flirt with it. If authentic prayer brings us to the throne, flirting keeps us in the courtyard.

A few years ago, we seemed to be living our dream. After a sixteen-year walk in the wilderness, we finally entered our professional promised land. Bobby had made it to the ranks of the major leagues as a baseball player relatively quickly. He was a first-round draft pick at the end of our junior year of college, and after a mere two years in the minor leagues, he found himself donning the pinstripes of the New York Yankees. He played for ten years (both in the major and minor leagues) before hanging up his spikes and joining the fraternity of professional coaches.

We naively assumed his trek to the majors as a coach would be similar to his experience as a player, but coaching was an entirely different story. We wallowed in the minors year after year, hoping to get our coveted break back onto a major-league field. During this time, I taught school and picked up odd jobs in the summers, while Bobby coached in small towns across the country and worked for a landscaping company during his off season. When we were finally invited to join the major-league staff of the Florida Marlins, we were ecstatic. We threw a major-league celebration at our home, complete with hot dogs, peanuts, Cracker Jack, and a cake the size of a small putting green!

The next year led to another big league invitation to coach first base for the San Diego Padres. We were thrilled to go back to the hometown of our beloved college, San Diego State University, so off we flew to southern California. But it was the following year that we felt God had wildly outdone himself in the "dreams come true" department. We were asked to join the staff of the New York Yankees as their third base coach. They offered twice the salary we were making in San Diego, and it took us all of one second to say yes to the New York invitation.

In addition to Bobby's dreams coming true, mine were shaping up too, as I was finally able to leave the confines of my classroom to pursue my twenty-year-old dream to write and speak in full-time ministry. My cry to God for the previous few years had been, "Lord, either tame me or unleash me, but I can't continue in this current state much longer." A full unleashing seemed to be happening before our eyes, and we playfully bounced our way through that year in New York.

But on a soggy October day, one week after a successful season of coaching was in the record books, we received a call from the Yankees general manager. "Bobby, it makes me sick to have to tell you this, but we're going to have to let you go." Our frazzled minds tried to understand this lunacy as he explained that a person within the organization had been lobbying to get Bobby fired. It was someone Bobby and I had prayed for the entire season as he flailed in a blitz of media frenzy over his marriage and character away from the ballpark.

To make matters worse, because Bobby and I vowed to handle this disappointment with integrity, Bobby decided to decline interviews from reporters clamoring for some insight into why he got fired. For months after this fated phone call we had no job and little hope as he seemed to be shunned from the society of baseball. When people don't know truth, they tend to make it up, and we fell victim to the hungering minds and mouths of falsehood.

Finally, about two weeks before the start of spring training, we got a call from the Philadelphia Phillies. They wanted to offer us an opportunity but almost seemed embarrassed to mention it. The job they had available was buried deep in their minor-league system. As a matter of fact, it was about as low as they go, plummeting Bobby from one of the best jobs in the country, serving as third base coach for the New York Yankees, to serving as a hitting coach in short-season single A ball — a place where our after-game meal was a loaf of white bread and a jar of peanut butter, with a tongue depressor used for a knife.

It was during this time that Bobby and I cemented the difference between authentic prayer and worry prayer in our fragile minds. Initially, my prayers during this period sounded like this: "Oh my goodness, Lord, we have no money. We are in debt up to our eyeballs with college payments and everyday expenses. We are going to lose our house. It's over. We're toast. In Jesus' name. Amen."

In worry prayer there's no real asking. No real praying. Just worry, spiced with a sprinkle of despair. Worry doesn't ask for anything; it just frets over everything.

I was stunned to find that tucked in the middle of one of the most quoted verses on prayer, Jesus offers a cure for anxiety. If these verses are dubbed the cure, I know I need the medicine he prescribes.

"Therefore I tell you, do not worry about your life, what you will eat or drink; or about your body, what you will wear. Is not life more than food, and the body more than clothes? Look at the birds of the air; they do not sow or reap or store away in barns, and yet your heavenly Father feeds them. Are you not much more valuable than they? Can any one of you by worrying add a single hour to your life?"

Matthew 6:25 – 27

Jesus teaches that being anxious is a waste of time. Even birds with brains the size of a pea know how to trust their Father. Truthfully, I've never seen a bird with its wing rubbing its head in a panicky sweat, so why do I act that way?

If we take Jesus' cure, we will fly free of our stash of worries. But we may need a little truth to push it out of the nest. Thankfully, Jesus doesn't proclaim, "Don't worry," and then leave us on our own to figure it out. In a brilliant transfusion of faith, he leads us from a place of worry to a haven of hope. This hope is propelled by *asking* in prayer instead of *fretting* in despair.

> "*Ask* and it will be given to you; *seek* and you will find; *knock* and the door will be opened to you. For everyone who asks receives; the one who seeks finds; and to the one who knocks, the door will be opened."
>
> Matthew 7:7 – 8, emphasis mine

Asking, seeking, and knocking sound easy enough, but the truth is that this progression of prayer is really a continuum for maturity, and maturity never seems to come without bumps and battle scars. It could be said that if asking starts us in prayer, then seeking confuses us and knocking downright irritates us. We want things quick and convenient; in the words of Burger King, we want to "have it *our* way!"

Asking is the most basic, surface place of prayer. It is the essential starting point for engaging God, and it is how our Spirit hunger begins to get fed. We present ourselves in a humble state as we enter into a type of spiritual stutter. We request and release, request and release, as we transfer our desires, hopes, needs, pain, and glory to God. This exchange fluctuates, depending on the depth of the circumstance, but asking is where it begins.

One would think that the asking stage of prayer would be easy, but ironically, many of us have hidden wounds that prevent us from freely asking God for things. These barriers can isolate us from this initial stage of asking:

- We don't understand God intimately.
- We aren't sure of God's good intent.
- We are afraid we aren't important enough.
- We have something in our past we aren't sure is forgiven.

INTIMACY'S CARESS

Intimacy with God is the gift that keeps on giving. There is nothing like it, and no substitute for it. But for many, a love for God is far away and stoic, like a statue in an empty cathedral.

When I was nine years old, an event in my family literally changed the trajectory of our lives. My dad was the youngest bank president in the state of Colorado. At the age of thirty-three, to all appearances he had the job, family, and charisma to light up any room he entered, but he also struggled with habits that were ripping apart his life. Drinking and disappearing were tearing my mom's heart out, and finally she had had enough. One night, my dad was returning home from the bank on the hilly roads that connect the city of Boulder to our suburb outside of Denver. His car went off the road and rolled several times, and a milkman found him many hours later, his body stretched over the front seat to the back. He was paralyzed from the neck down. Now my heartbroken mom had to stand by the bedside of her injured husband, trying to imagine a life of wheelchair ramps and bedsores, while images of a marriage badly broken before the fateful wreck loomed in the front of her memories.

My father spent six months in the intensive care unit and another six months at Craig Rehabilitation Center. During this time, my Grandma McGuire would fly in from Maryland to take care of us. I have often thought I had the best grandmothers in the world. One lived in a small mountain town tucked in the snowcapped slopes of Colorado, while the other was from the nation's capital, a born and bred East Coast lady.

Grandma McGuire tried to teach me about prayer after my dad's accident, but I would have no part of it. She gathered my little sister and brother on my bed at night, while I ran into the bathroom and locked the door, screaming from my seat on top of the toilet that if God was worth praying to, then why did he let my dad end up paralyzed and my mom distraught and ensnared by vodka? In my nine-year-old mind, praying just didn't seem to make sense. But each night she continued to gather my siblings, and I continued to take my seat on the toilet.

I could hear them in my room reciting prayers like the Our Father and creeds like the Apostles' Creed, and I finally decided to have some words with this God my grandmother believed in. I simply said things like, "Help us, Jesus. We're in trouble, God. How are we going to make it? Protect my little sister and brother." As they recited their prayers, I quietly mumbled my own.

This pattern continued every time my grandmother would come for her extended visits. As the years passed, I found myself walking to church to be a part of the Scripture readings and being drawn to a God I didn't know or understand.

I remember a conversation with my grandma several years later that I will always treasure. She struggled with seasons of depression and was beginning to feel herself slipping into the darkness. One morning I crawled into bed with her as she was clutching her prayer book and praying a string of recited prayers. I whispered to her that I now understood how to pray. That God had opened my heart and spirit to his love. I shared that she could simply speak to him rather than chant rehearsed prayers. As we held each other in a tender embrace, she spoke words to God that came from the core of who she was. She looked at me, the wrinkles of time and grace etched across her creased face, and wept as she said, "In all my life I've never done that. I never knew I could speak to him with words that come from my heart."

Intimacy with God doesn't come from religious fortitude; it comes from authentic engagement. His heart wrapped in mine in an intimacy that isn't forced or faked, but is real and transcendent.

Do I Matter?

Many women I speak to are regular churchgoers who truly love God, but they are hesitant to engage God in prayer because they feel like they've gotten burned in the asking phase.

"I prayed for healing, and my friend passed away."

"I've prayed for a child, and we still struggle with infertility."

"I pray to be free of my habits and compulsions, but I seem to stay stuck in the midst of destruction."

A sense of *asking without receiving* permeates this viewpoint. It slowly chips away at Jesus' appeal to us to ask.

While some feel burned by their petitions, others cower, afraid to ask because of a sense of not being important enough to have an audience with God. "He's got more important things to worry about than my desire for a husband," or "My illness isn't as bad as what the earthquake victims just endured." In God's family there is no ranking when it comes to the importance of your asking prayers. Whenever you ask, God thrills to listen.

Jesus continues to explain the importance of asking by describing God's attitude toward our prayers.

> "Which of you, if your son asks for bread, will give him a stone? Or if he asks for a fish, will give him a snake? If you, then, though you are evil, know how to give good gifts to your children, how much more will your Father in heaven give good gifts to those who ask him!"
>
> Matthew 7:9 – 11

Jesus is either on target with his plea for us to ask, or he is a liar. He is either good, or he is selectively playing favorites. God's intent in our lives is always right and always noble. He answers every prayer we utter, even if we struggle to interpret the answers with our limited capacity for perfect knowledge. Each of our requests ranks an explanation point in its importance and relevance to him.

AM I FORGIVEN?

There is a commonality that spills over those of us with Spirit hunger: we struggle to forgive ourselves and let go of the past. Addictions, abortions, past sexual liaisons, relationships we've tried to salvage, and even conversations continue to haunt us. Old events hold on like a fake hug from an unwelcome adversary.

Whenever we sense a faint murmur in our minds that we aren't really forgiven, we view the act of engaging God in prayer a little like watering dead grass — futile and pointless. Our minds counter any hope we have by shamefully whispering, "I'll pray, but I don't deserve to be heard."

My friend Trista was the picture of confidence. Gorgeous, talented, and a lover of God, she seemed to glide through life with ease and purpose. One day as we talked, she got strangely silent, and soon tears splashed down her perfectly blushed cheeks. She shared with me that over a decade earlier she had made a choice to end a pregnancy. A husband and four kids later, she still felt chained to the guilt she had begged Jesus to remove. "I'm not worthy to pray," she sobbed. "It's a wonder God tolerates me, let alone blesses me with answered prayer." I held her tightly and assured her of God's astounding forgiveness. She had heard it hundreds of times, but that day was different. She longed to move past prayer cloaked in guilt to prayer wrapped in hope.

If we're clinging to the notion that we have to be flawless to be heard, we need to realize that nothing could be further from the truth. We view the grass of our guilty hearts as dead, but God doesn't. He sees us as alive and worthy. Vibrant and new. Whatever we're holding on to in the sin department, he has already dismissed and forgotten. If we've expressed a "soul sorrow" for our behavior, God makes us clean and fresh like new linen on a crisply made bed. Our prayers are welcomed and treasured by a God who loves to meet us where we are.

ASKING POSTURES

The fact that Jesus explicitly instructs us to *ask* is evident. It's not an option that he offers; it's a directive he commands. But how we posture ourselves in the asking can make a difference. Consider the postures of petitioning in these two accounts from the gospel of Luke.

The Posture of Flesh Healing

In the first encounter, Jesus is traveling between Samaria and Galilee. This is a little like traveling between Las Vegas and a Bible-believing town in the South — different people and different belief systems. But one thing that doesn't change is the fellowship of suffering, which a group of interfaith lepers could attest to.

> As he was going into a village, ten men who had leprosy met him. They stood at a distance and called out in a loud voice, "Jesus, Master, have pity on us!"
>
> When he saw them, he said, "Go, show yourselves to the priests." And as they went, they were cleansed.
>
> One of them, when he saw he was healed, came back, praising God in a loud voice. He threw himself at Jesus' feet and thanked him — and he was a Samaritan.
>
> Jesus asked, "Were not all ten cleansed? Where are the other nine? Has no one returned to give praise to God except this foreigner?" Then he said to him, "Rise and go; your faith has made you well."
>
> Luke 17:12 – 19

As these ten scarred men stood on the side of the road, screaming to a Master they weren't sure would hear, it seemed their bandaged lives took a turn for good as Jesus stopped to address their pain. He didn't promise them healing; he just told them to go and show themselves to the priests. Going to see a priest was like going to see a doctor in their day. The priests had the power to accept them back into society or to continue a banishment decree over their infected lives.

Miraculously, as they walked toward the town that had shunned them, all of them were cleansed! Raw flesh made new. Torn skin made whole. The bandages covering shameful limbs were now flying in the wind. You'd think they would immediately sprint to the One who proclaimed this new verdict over their lives, but sadly, only one returned to glorify the giver.

As he galloped to the feet of this Master, he screamed out in a loud voice, "Thank you! Thank you! It's unbelievable!" Then he fell at Jesus' feet and worshiped, uttering the deep sighs of gratitude that only those healed from shame and despair can understand.

Jesus was surprised that this foreigner was the only one who came back to express his joy after his "asking" had been fulfilled. All too often we ask and receive and are already on to the next petition instead of screaming and shouting thanks in a loud voice. It's a posture of *flesh healing* but not *heart filling*. Who cares if our flesh is healed if our hearts aren't filled with a new sense of awe toward the healer?

The Posture of Showing Up

Tucked in the gospel of Luke is another posture of petitioning so tender it may break your heart. Jesus was teaching in one of the synagogues on the Sabbath, and a woman was listening, a woman who for eighteen years had struggled with a sickness "caused by a spirit." Luke, a physician by trade, described this woman as being bent over double, unable to straighten up at all. Can you imagine a woman not even able to look up, spending her days parallel to the floor?

When Jesus saw this woman, he called her over and spoke healing over her curved life and spine:

"Woman, you are freed from your sickness."
     And He laid His hands on her; and immediately she was made erect again and began glorifying God.

But the synagogue official, indignant because Jesus had healed on the Sabbath, began saying to the crowd in response, "There are six days in which work should be done; so come during them and get healed, and not on the Sabbath day."

But the Lord answered him and said, "You hypocrites, does not each of you on the Sabbath untie his ox or his donkey from the stall and lead him away to water him? And this woman, a daughter of Abraham as she is, whom Satan has bound for eighteen long years, should she not have been released from this bond on the Sabbath day?"

As He said this, all His opponents were being humiliated; and the entire crowd was rejoicing over all the glorious things being done by Him.

Luke 13:12–17 NASB

I love the posture of this broken woman. Her life and back are bent over. She can't even look Jesus in the eye when he calls her to come, but she bends next to him when he calls her, and the posture of just showing up begins to pay off.

She has struggled for eighteen years with this mess, and by the command of Jesus, at just the right time in her history and the history of those watching, her life straightens out.

She began glorifying God, and so did all those around her who chose the authentic, powerful movement of a living God rather than a squelching religious tradition. This is an asking petition that bellows with promise. *Just show up. Even if your life is bent over double.*

What if this precious woman hadn't kept showing up at the synagogue? What if she had grown tired of the belief that God could change her life, her body, her attitude? She would have missed her straightening moment with the Savior, the new posture that she now shared with a parched, bent world.

Asking is where we begin. Sometimes it takes the form of asking from the side of the road, as the lepers did, and taking the time to relish God's movement when he brings about change. And sometimes it takes the form of simply nudging up next to him so he can straighten our bent backs. Asking is the place we start.

chapter 6

—

BANGING ON DOORS

One of the most direct ways God speaks to us in the seeking phase of prayer is through the Bible. If you're rolling your eyes right now with a "been there, done that" sigh, let me put a fresh hug of encouragement around your neck. I don't care how mature we are in our faith or how many times we've tried to read and felt like we've heard nothing — the Bible is filled with a wisdom we will be unraveling until we take our last breath here on earth.

I have times when I pick up my Bible, begging God for answers to things I'm seeking, and feel like I'm taking a mere garden hoe to a massive mound of doubt. Why don't I hear from God like other people do? Can he really speak to my current situation from an ancient text?

One of the complaints I hear is, "I don't feel like God answers my prayers. I don't feel like I hear from him." I typically respond by asking, "What kind of time do you spend reading his Word?" The answer is usually a sheepish "not much." Although Bible reading is not the only way we get direction from God, it is a huge part of the precise answers we beg for when we need help.

In the seeking phase, it's important to write down the things we sense God is saying. Journals, laptops, iPads, or the pages of plain note-books can become the backdrop for your sacred seeking.

I shared earlier that my marriage was in trouble. Actually, it was swirling around in the toilet bowl, about to be flushed, but God had different plans. I decided I needed time away from Bobby to sort through the pain that unfaithfulness had brought to my marriage, so we separated for several months. I had three small kids, a full-time job, and a load of pain so great that the back of my head went numb. At one point the doctors actually thought I had a brain tumor.

One day after work, I called my babysitter to see if she could stay a little longer so I could drive somewhere to have a moaning session with God. I drove into the foothills and settled next to a stream that gurgled alongside a purple meadow of wildflowers. "Beauty next to ashes," I whispered, as I mulled over my charred thoughts. "Is our marriage going to make it? Should I stay with this man I love, hating what he has done to our vows? Can we ever rebuild trust?"

As I sat on a rock next to this clear stream, I saw a vision in my head of a new wedding. A ceremony with fresh vows and new rings. I also saw us standing before an audience of professional athletes, giving God the credit for gluing the shattered pieces of our lives back together.

"Wait a minute," I thought. "I'm just creating this in my head because I want it so badly." I prayed for truth like never before. Our family was standing on the brink of disaster, and I needed immediate intervention.

With pen in hand, I began jotting down my vision and hope for a new marriage and future with Bobby. For months I prayed, studied, wrote, and cried. We had to crawl out of dark caves, but we had a lantern — the Bible — and our Lord as our guide.

Bobby and I renewed our vows later that year, just the two of us and a pastor we loved. We had new rings on our fingers and hope in our hearts, but it wasn't until this past year that I fell to my knees in awe of what God had done.

I was asked to speak at a conference of professional athletes and their wives. Bobby and I loved every minute of our time with these precious couples, and as the conference neared its end, the last session knocked me over. An open microphone was available for anyone who wanted to talk about what God was stirring up in their lives. Being a professional speaker and a natural talker, I was going to sit this one out. I had talked enough. Bobby looked over at me and whispered, "We need to go up there."

I followed Bobby onto the stage, where he took the microphone and began sharing. He talked about our marriage and how God had rebuilt it from the garbage heap. He talked about the healing in his life and the ensuing maturity. And then he spoke to all the women in the crowd. You could have heard a pin drop on the carpet, it was so intense. He said, "Ladies, I want you to know that even if we don't act like it, we need you. We are weak. God gives you to us to make us stronger, and without you, we are nothing." In front of some of the strongest athletes in the game of baseball, Bobby turned to me and pledged his love to me.

I was speechless — a miracle in itself. I looked out over the crowd and couldn't stop crying as I thought about the vision and prayer I had recorded fifteen years earlier by the stream. I never want to sugarcoat anything in God's kingdom. Marriages are hard and sometimes fail. We hope and pray for certain outcomes in our lives, and sometimes God takes us on paths that we wouldn't choose — but the end is still the same. God knows. When we seek him, we will find him. And it's usually in the confusion of seeking that we find.

Does God Have a Plan?

This is where prayer gets messy. Seeking is the place where we have to get our hands in the mud and get dirty because the answers may not be clean and clear. People often talk about "God's plan" as if humanity lies down on a giant appointment book and folds into the pages as they turn. Cold and calculated, our plans can dictate unbending time frames and expected outcomes. But the plans of God aren't packaged like this. As a matter of fact, they aren't packaged at all. God uniquely guides, directs, and allows the circumstances of our lives to drive us to a place of seeking. We seek his wisdom. We seek his purpose. We seek his will.

It's in the seeking stage of prayer that we ask for an illuminated answer from God or simply a quiet nudge in a particular direction. When things we seek seem about as clear as mud, thankfully there are some things we can be certain *are* his will.

God is a God of redemption (2 Peter 3:9). If you've been praying for someone to understand God's love and to transfer the reins of their life to God's capable hands, you can rest assured that his desire for their life is the same as yours. There's the sticky matter of free will, where each person we pray for has the right to say yes or no to God's love invitation, but because of God's character and essence, he wants to redeem everyone's life. This is especially comforting to those of us who have prayed for a long time for someone, only to see them continue to wallow in their mire or stay stuck in their mud. We can be sure God's will always bends toward redemption and redefined lives.

We can be free (John 8:36). Sometimes people comment, "I think this habit or addiction is just the cross I have to bear in this life." I firmly say, "No, it's not! If that were true, Jesus wouldn't have talked so emphatically about freedom." Taking up our cross and following him refers to a faith commitment, not a slavery indictment. Behaviors we feel trapped by are things Jesus died to set us free from. His death enables our freedom.

We can have peace (John 14:27). Circumstances may shift, but God doesn't. We are protected by his peace, a peace that transcends human understanding, even if we are in the midst of confusion or chaos. Peace is the comfort that looks confusion in the face and gently smiles. God fills us with the assurance that he is bigger than our circumstances.

We don't have to be afraid (Psalm 145:18 – 19). One of the by-products of the seeking phase of prayer can be fear. When we seek and don't see, we often fall prey to fear. Over and over, the Bible assures us that we don't have to be afraid. When we are in the thick of difficult circumstances, reaching out to God and praying for his will and direction, we see only what is in front of us; God sees the horizon. We see with limited perspective; he sees with unlimited wisdom. We handle one puzzle piece, while he sees the finished puzzle.

If you've been seeking God's will in these areas of your life — redemption, freedom, peace, fear — the answer you can count on from God is "Yes, I will redeem!" "Yes, you can be free!" "Yes, I give you peace!" "No, you do not have to be afraid!"

But what about when we seek God's will in more specific terms? "Do I take this job?" "Do we move to this house or that house?" "What school should my kids go to?" "Is this the best doctor for me?"

The Bible's most quoted verse when it comes to seeking has to be Jeremiah 29:11. It seems to be engraved on more coffee mugs, plaques, and postcards than any other Scriptures combined.

"For I know the plans I have for you," declares the LORD, "plans to prosper you and not to harm you, plans to give you hope and a future."

Although I love this portion of Scripture, the words that follow this popular verse hold the punch:

"Then you will call upon Me and come and pray to Me, and I will listen to you. You will seek Me and find Me when you search for Me with all your heart."

Jeremiah 29:12 – 13 NASB

God has plans for our lives, and the plans are good — that's his part. But now look at our part: we call on him, pray to him, listen, seek, and search with all that is within us. This is the seeking phase of prayer.

The Tenacity of Knocking

There's a sliver of Scripture between the Lord's Prayer and our wrestling with asking, seeking, and knocking that makes me chuckle. Here Jesus addresses the irritating nature of the knocking phase of prayer:

> "Suppose you have a friend, and you go to him at midnight and say, 'Friend, lend me three loaves of bread; a friend of mine on a journey has come to me, and I have no food to offer him.' And suppose the one inside answers, "Don't bother me. The door is already locked, and my children and I are in bed. I can't get up and give you anything.' I tell you, even though he will not get up and give you the bread because of friendship, yet because of your shameless audacity he will surely get up and give you as much as you need."

> Luke 11:5 – 8

In Jesus' time, people often lived in close quarters. They shared a common area with doors that separated rooms in which families would sleep. In this passage, one of the friends has the nerve to go banging on his neighbor's door late at night. To make matters worse, he is asking for food to feed friends! I've often wondered why this man bothered his neighbor for food at such a late hour. Wouldn't sleep have been a greater priority, with the plan of asking for breakfast in the morning more reasonable? Seemingly oblivious of the time or the snores coming from his neighbor's hovel, he bangs. I can just hear the man shouting back, "Are you serious? Get lost!"

But he doesn't get lost, and Jesus tells us it wasn't because they were friends that the man finally got up to give him some food, it was because he was *persistent*. The neighbor kept knocking until he finally got an answer.

What does this say about persistence? Are we supposed to start banging on people's doors, screaming for help until we arouse someone?

I believe Jesus is trying to illuminate a concept that we struggle to digest — the concept of tenacity. *Tenacity* is a word that has more energy than *endurance*. Enduring makes me tired, while tenacity fills me with vitality.

Oswald Chambers defines tenacity as "the absolute certainty that what we are looking for is going to transpire."[7] In prayer, this means we stick with what we pray for with a fortitude coated in courage. Hope saturated in belief. Staying power fueled by certainty.

Think about the time period that passes as we knock on someone's door. We arrive at the door and knock about four times. We wait about thirty seconds before knocking again. After those long seconds pass, we repeat — knock, knock, knock, knock. Another thirty seconds ticks by. We look around and possibly, if we're nosy, peek into a window. After a total of about sixty seconds, we determine that no one is home.

Often this is the way we pray. We ask for something. We wait for a short period of time. We ask again (seek), hoping to get a response. We ask one last time, and then we leave, thinking there's no one home and we won't get an answer. Rarely do we even make it to the knocking stage that demands a measure of tenacity and persistence to see it through.

Knocking is where we grow up in prayer. It perseveres until the impossible becomes the possible. In prayer we need to keep knocking until we get an answer, or until we're released from praying that prayer. God always answers our prayers. Always! He answers in one of three ways:

1. **Yes.** Doors open, and you know God has opened them up for you to walk through.

2. **No.** When God answers no to a request, either he is protecting you from something or he has something better in mind.

3. **Coming soon.** If you're in a "coming soon" phase, know that God is working in the present time frame for outcomes in your future. This is a matter of timing, so obediently continue to pray with tenacity and belief.

Praying with tenacity became real for me after we lost our job with the Yankees. I shared how my prayers were marked by worry with "God words" sitting like bookends at the beginning and end of my prayers. After we took a minor-league job with the Philadelphia Phillies, things really got dicey. I put tenacity to the test as I vowed to let worry prayers die. I stood with veracity on the notion that seeking and knocking were going to take me to a new maturity in prayer.

Bobby and I left our home in Colorado to spend the baseball season in Williamsport, Pennsylvania — home to the mighty Crosscutters. Our mascot was a giant varmint with a saw in his hand.

We were thankful to rent a place close to the tiny stadium, and as it turned out, we stayed in a house that during the school year was divided into two apartments to house college students. The furniture was so dirty that Bobby put sheets over the couch and chairs. I've rarely laughed so hard as when I saw him take a seat on the couch and his torso literally disappear into the cushions, making his hands and legs look like those of a preschool child. No air conditioning in the hot summer humidity, no washing machine, and a moldy bathroom. I decided to take my sad heart and plunge it into some serious housecleaning. Windex in hand, I started to wash one of the filmy windows when the entire window, wooden frame and all, fell out of the sill, smacked me in the head, and cut my forehead! Blood streaming down my face, I sat on the floor and cried. *"God, what good can possibly come from this? Haven't we already paid our dues in baseball? We are moving away from your will instead of toward it!"*

I gave myself a two-minute period to feel self-pity and then picked myself up and went to sit in the creaky old stadium and cheer our team on.

That season held more treasure than a sunken pirate ship. Bobby and I decided we were seriously going to entreat God about restoring us to the major leagues, so we decided to fast and pray every Monday. We had never done anything like that before, so the waters were a bit uncharted, but we dedicated Mondays to seeking and finding, to knocking and looking for openings. Our son, Colton, a college baseball player, joined us midseason to rehabilitate his arm after surgery. This time together was revealing as I watched him study his father like a hawk. One Monday as the three of us were praying, Colton uttered words that had Bobby and me in tears: "Thank you, Lord, for letting me watch how my dad handles disappointment. I see how he treats the players on this team and the young head coach who tries to lead, and I'm learning what it means to trust you even when we'd rather be somewhere else."

I traveled with that team to every small town in the Northeast. As the season crawled to an end, we left the Crosscutters with no leads for a better job and with financial ruin close on our heels if things didn't change.

On an October weekend, I went to be the guest speaker at a women's retreat on prayer. Bobby decided to spend the weekend fasting and praying about his job. While we still hadn't seen any change in circumstances, his heart and mine were resting in the belief that God was stirring something. In desperate need for more financial stability, I had returned to my old consulting job and resumed a schedule filled with travel. While I was away in northern California, I got a call from Bobby saying that the Houston Astros were in the market to hire a new manager, and one of our good friends was a candidate for the job.

In itself this was wildly miraculous because for six months Bobby kept saying, "I think the Houston Astros would be a good fit for us." I would respond, "Sure, and so would a spot in the White House!" That's how impossible it seemed.

The Astros had extended a contract to their current staff during the season, guaranteeing their jobs for another year — which meant there were virtually no job openings for this team, but this didn't derail Bobby who kept praying expectantly as our minor-league season crept to an end.

With a new surge of excitement we prayed, but we knew ten other candidates were interviewing for the same position. Bobby was confident our guy had a good chance as the field narrowed from ten men to two.

On a windy day in late October, our friend was named the manager of the Houston Astros, and he asked Bobby to join his staff as his first base coach. We were breathless at this turn of events. Ironically, that same week, the Phillies clinched a World Series spot against the Yankees and wanted to fly all of their coaches in for a weekend of play-off games and galas. We were committed to the Astros for the next year, but the Phillies insisted we join them for the World Series games. After a long season with the saw-carrying Crosscutters, we were happy to go.

The first night there, we attended a formal party with personnel from both the Phillies and the Yankees when we heard a familiar voice. It was the general manager of the New York Yankees, the same man who had fired Bobby a year earlier. He gave each of us a hug and then spoke some of the sweetest words we had ever heard. "Bobby," he said, "last week the Astros called to ask what kind of a man you are. I told them you're the classiest guy in the game. The way you handled yourself after you got fired was the classiest thing I've seen."

Bobby and I couldn't wait to get out of that crowded place and debrief on what had just happened. God had taken us to the job we thought was the pinnacle of where we wanted to be, allowed us to plummet from that place, and then taken us to a new place that held even greater purpose and reward.

Asking, seeking, and knocking lead us to maturity, and maturity leads us to the face of Jesus. If we don't ask, we won't receive. If we don't seek, our lives won't be opened. And if we don't knock, we'll stay stuck in the confines of shallow belief.

chapter 7

—

PANTING
AND PETITION

I've never considered myself to be a good cook. As a matter of fact, I think my family would tell you that toast and scrambled eggs sit at the top of my culinary specialties. The other day, I was looking over the menu at a fun Italian restaurant, wondering how someone could come up with ten distinctive types of pasta when it dawned on me: Prayer is a lot like pasta. Spaghetti, rigatoni, penne, and lasagna have different shapes but are still made from the base of a noodle. So it is with prayer. Panting and petition take many forms, but they all bubble up from a yearning for God.

Trying to define types of prayer seems a bit like trying to name blades of grass. How do we begin to distinguish the heart cries and moans — the joy and revelation that prayer brings to our lives?

It's here that we look at prayer through different lenses. The enormity of trying to define prayer can either overwhelm us or encourage us to bite off nibbles our Spirit hunger can digest.

BREATH PRAYER

The apostle Paul urged the Thessalonians to pray without ceasing, but I've always struggled to understand what this might look like in our everyday lives. Do we walk around robotically praising God as we bounce from activity to activity in our crowded days? Or do we retreat to a quiet, spa-like atmosphere and kidnap our minds, forcing ourselves to stop thinking and start praying? Oswald Chambers writes this:

> If we think of prayer as the breath in our lungs and the blood from our hearts, we think rightly. The blood flows ceaselessly, and the breathing continues ceaselessly; we are not conscious of it, but it is always going on. We are not always conscious of Jesus keeping us in perfect joint with God, but if we are obeying him, he always is. Prayer is not an exercise, it is the life.[8]

If prayer can be as natural as breathing, why does it seem to take so much effort? Why do our minds scatter and our words mumble? I have found help in my pursuit of a ceaseless prayer life in the notion of *breath prayer*.

Breath prayer really has its roots in the Psalms, where a phrase might be repeated over and over to focus the mind on a particular idea. David was a master of breath prayer as he uttered such phrases as "the Lord is my shepherd"; "delight yourself in the Lord"; "Lord, you are my Rock and my salvation." Sometimes it seems as though David is whispering to himself, inviting God into a prayerful tryst that only the two of them can understand. Like breathing, the rhythm of this type of prayer redirects and refocuses a wandering mind or heart that needs to be reassured.

One night I was driving to the ballpark to watch a baseball game. Our team had just been sold to a new owner for more than 600 million dollars. Rumors were flying that he was going to bring in a whole new staff to usher our last-place team to a place of significance in the standings. Having uprooted everything to move to Houston, with my dream of writing and speaking flourishing in this new city, nerves and tension tightened in me as I drove. Breath prayers began to swell, spilling out as breath before the Lord: "My Savior, remove my fear"; "Lord Jesus, help me to see your purpose"; "Sweet Jesus, cleanse me from all doubt"; "Abba Father, you are my confidence."

Short and sweet, this type of prayer asks for comfort and the kiss of assurance. It's the perfect ointment to a wandering mind that is prone to get distracted or pulled into the pit of despair.

Richard Foster guides us into discovering breath prayer for ourselves:

- Sit in silence, being held in God's presence.
- Allow God to call you by name.
- Allow God to ask you, "What do you want?" "What is stirring within you?"
- Perhaps a single word will surface — peace, faith, courage, hope, inspiration.
- Maybe a phrase will come to mind — "to understand your truth" or "to feel your love."
- Connect the word or phrase to a comfortable way you express your praise to God — Savior, Abba, my Father, sweet Lord.
- Say the prayer within the confines of a single breath.[9]

A woman approached me recently, gushing, "I love this type of prayer. I've been praying like this and didn't even know it." She continued. "My favorite breath prayer is *faith, not fear — sweet Jesus — faith, not fear.*" I am so glad she shared her prayer with me, because I've literally uttered those words repeatedly over the last few days.

This type of prayer is refreshing because it keeps redirecting our minds. Like the cadence of short breaths, it hushes and quiets a noisy head. Some breath prayers stay with me for weeks, while I may pray others for just a day. When my mind wanders in my attempts at prayer, I use this to rein it back in.

BREAKTHROUGH PRAYER

Breakthrough prayer is the kind of prayer that stirs things up. While breath prayer centers more around comfort and focus, this is the kind of prayer that says, "I can't accept things the way they are for one more minute! I have to have a breakthrough."

One of the best examples of this type of prayer is seen in the life of a desperate woman named Hannah. She was married to a man who had two wives, already an invitation to a heap of insecurity. On top of this, Hannah couldn't get pregnant, and her rival wife had a quiver full of children! Each year they would travel to Shiloh, where they would worship and sacrifice to the Lord.

> Whenever the day came for Elkanah to sacrifice, he would give portions of the meat to his wife Peninnah and to all her sons and daughters. But to Hannah he gave a double portion because he loved her, and the LORD had closed her womb. Because the LORD had closed Hannah's womb, her rival kept provoking her in order to irritate her. This went on year after year. Whenever Hannah went up to the house of the LORD, her rival provoked her till she wept and would not eat.
>
> 1 Samuel 1:4 – 7

Ironically, both of these women suffered from having to share their husband. Peninnah chose to be mean and bitter, turning her hurt and heartache into a voice full of irritating comments and taunts. Hannah just shut down, crying and not eating. Year after year, she watched the same disappointing scene play out like a bad television rerun.

Finally her husband seemed to notice that Hannah was beside herself, and he clumsily asked her several questions:

> "Hannah, why are you weeping? Why don't you eat? Why are you downhearted? Don't I mean more to you than ten sons?"
>
> 1 Samuel 1:8

Obviously this was a man who couldn't understand the "mother heart" of a woman. I can imagine what she may have said under her breath to him after that careless statement: "As a matter of fact, you *aren't* better than ten sons!" But instead of provoking a fight, something changes in Hannah. She did get up and eat and then went to the temple.

> In her deep anguish Hannah prayed to the LORD, weeping bitterly.
>
> 1 Samuel 1:10

We don't know anything about Hannah prior to this story, so we don't know if prayer was something she typically engaged in, but now it's as though some bold, new initiative has taken over her life. Distressed and bawling, she is ushering in a breakthrough with God.

> And she made a vow, saying, "LORD Almighty, if you will only look on your servant's misery and remember me, and not forget your servant but give her a son, then I will give him to the LORD for all the days of his life, and no razor will ever be used on his head."
>
> 1 Samuel 1:11

This is dangerously bold prayer. It's the type of prayer uttered when hope looks a bright shade of black. Some people think Hannah was bargaining with God much like a sailor capsized at sea, who says, "If you rescue me, God, I promise to live for you." The problem with capsized prayer is that once a person is rescued, the fervor of the prayer is soon forgotten. Hannah's plea for a breakthrough is much deeper than a capsized prayer. In fact, she prays so wildly, so desperately, that the priest Eli thinks she is drunk. Mixed within the salty tears of a desperate woman is a priest who is clueless.

> Then Eli said to her, "How long will you make yourself drunk? Put away your wine from you."
> But Hannah replied, "No, my lord, I am a woman oppressed in spirit; I have drunk neither wine nor strong drink, but I have poured out my soul before the LORD." ...
> Then Eli answered and said, "Go in peace; and may the God of Israel grant your petition that you have asked of Him."
>
> 1 Samuel 1:14 – 15, 17 NASB

Hannah is at the end of her rope. She has been hanging on by a thread and is at a point where only a breakthrough with the Lord will do. If we listen to the tone of her prayer, it has the spunk of "*If you ..., then I.*" It's more about her heart and her commitment than about *what* she is praying. She is defining her belief in God by exclaiming, "I have poured out my soul before the Lord — and I will not leave here the same."

The stunning part of this prayer is how it trickled down into Hannah's countenance.

> So the woman went her way and ate, and her face was no longer sad.
>
> 1 Samuel 1:18 NASB

Hannah got her breakthrough with brilliant clarity. And although she wasn't pregnant yet, and she didn't know she would soon give birth to a son who would be one of the greatest prophets the world would ever know, she had peace. She was no longer sad.

This type of prayer has a process to it. It's not subtle or sudden, because breakthroughs are only necessary when there's been a buildup of pain and heartache over time. This type of pain craves the hope of a new beginning, a fresh start, a reshuffling of our "life cards." There is a process to breakthrough prayer that can't be mistaken.

PROCESS OF A BREAKTHROUGH

I am afflicted.

Remember me, Lord. Don't forget me.

I cry out my request.

I will have a role in this commitment.

I don't care who is watching.

I have been pushed to a point of desperation.

I am no longer sad. I have release as I trust you, Lord.

When we are at the end of our will, at the end of trying to control a set of circumstances, we are ready for breakthrough prayer. I've seen this kind of prayer change events and, more important, change me.

I can still recall my elation when I saw breakthrough prayer change the course of events in my family's life. After Bobby finished playing baseball, we slid into the role of coaching with no other real career options. Bobby had been drafted out of college and left without a degree, so when it came time to earn a living, his choices were limited. Although I had obtained a degree and a teaching certificate, I hadn't used it as we traversed the country with our moves over his ten-year career as a baseball player.

Not long into Bobby's new role as a minor-league coach, we sold our home in New York and headed to my home state of Colorado. After living in an apartment for a while, we found a cheap, small house we figured we would live in for no more than a year. Eight years later, we were still living in that house. The house itself wasn't horrible, but the years that passed in that house were marked by pain and a low-grade depression I couldn't seem to shake. It was in that house that our marriage fell apart, and rebuilding took place. The street we lived on had many rental properties, and the care of the homes plummeted further with each new tenant. The house next to ours once belonged to a couple who nursed the weeds out of their grass with Q-tips. When they sold the home, it passed through the hands of many renters who couldn't have cared less about it. Our back porch looked directly into our neighbor's backyard. Daily I would see several family members doing drugs out in the yard! This was not an acceptable place for our three elementary-aged kids to come home to, but we felt trapped because we couldn't afford to move out of the neighborhood.

With a mixture of bad memories from our wounded marriage and the stench of drugs coming from our backyard, I began to pray for a breakthrough. Every day, I would drive through a neighborhood that was near us but had a completely different feel. Well-kept homes, families playing out in the streets, and a neighborhood pool bursting with kids; this was the type of place I wanted my kids to grow up in. I drove the streets of that neighborhood for eight straight months and prayed. Sometimes I would get out of the car and pray over the blocks of homes as I walked. I even made a flyer with my contact information on it, as I rang doorbells asking if anyone was willing to sell their home.

One day, one of my friends called and said there was a house sitting empty in the neighborhood, and it happened to be on my favorite street. The woman who lived there suffered from Alzheimer's disease and had to leave the home. It sat abandoned for years after her son nearly destroyed it with reckless living during the years he resided there after his mother moved out. I quickly met with a realtor and got a quick tour of the inside of the home. Our realtor was a godly man who understood my language of faith and seemed to appreciate some of the crazy ways I went about finding this place. When we crunched the numbers, I fell into a panic as I quickly realized we would be in over our heads. Bobby was a minor-league coach and I was teaching school, but the down payment and monthly mortgage seemed out of our reach. Bobby was traveling from state to state with his team and had never actually seen the home, but he was trying to make this happen — like a favor you would do for someone you know needs a change. We were able to scrounge up a loan from my dad but still were falling short of what we needed to buy the house. I knew I was going to have to give it up.

I picked up the phone and called our realtor as tears spilled down my face. I thanked him for all the work he had done for us. I praised him for being a reflection of Jesus to me. I hung up the phone and sobbed. "Looks like I need to make the best of this home and just be thankful that I have one," I whispered.

The next day, the kids and I left to travel with Bobby. We spent the night in a small town in Kentucky as we traveled to meet the team on the East Coast. After dinner I went out for a walk, basking in the warm night air and enjoying the velvet black sky sprinkled with stars. I looked up and uttered a small prayer: "Lord, if we're meant to have this house, please save it for us. I've released it to you, and I'm not scrambling to grab it back. I just pray that if you mean to break through these circumstances, you will."

What happened next was breathtaking. The following morning as we were getting ready to leave the hotel, Bobby checked his voice mail. We were with the Pittsburgh Pirates at the time, and his team voice mail was rarely used for communication. For some reason, he felt compelled to check it that morning. His eyebrows raised as he mouthed to me, "How did our realtor get this number?" We were perplexed as he called him back. He explained to Bobby that he tracked down the Pirates' number through my mother in Colorado because he had something big to share with us. He said he had been thinking about our tearful conversation for two days, and he felt the Lord had showed him a way we could get that house! He offered to work with the seller's realtor to get the price down even further, and he was willing to skip his own commission, both on the sale of our current home and the purchase of the new one, to enable us to afford the home. In disbelief Bobby and I hung up the phone, fell to our knees, and cried. Not only did God get us into that home, but our family shared twelve richly blessed years there. I told our new neighbors that I could have literally kissed the bricks of that place because it was an answer to my breakthrough prayer.

Just when we think we can't take it any longer, God reveals himself either by the swift shifting of circumstances or by the gentle shift of our attitude toward them. Either way … it's a breakthrough.

DIRECTION PRAYER

Sometimes we need direction from God in a timely manner. We need to make decisions, or we need clear answers quickly for specific situations. David found himself engaging in this type of prayer when he was on the run from King Saul. He had been living in caves and in the forest as an unlikely crew of people joined him — those who were distressed, those in debt, and people hopelessly discontent with their lives. He became their leader, and during this time he developed what every good leader must possess at some point, the ability to make clear decisions in the face of uncertainty. David was informed that the Philistines, longtime enemies of God's people, were attacking the innocent people of Keilah and plundering their goods. David went straight to prayer for direction.

> He inquired of the LORD, saying, "Shall I go and attack these Philistines?"
>
> The Lord answered him, "Go, attack the Philistines and save Keilah."
>
> 1 Samuel 23:2

David's men weren't so sure David had heard correctly. They let him know they were scared enough out of their wits just hiding there in Judah, let alone going after the Philistines to protect the residents of this city. But David asked the same question again in prayer and got the same answer.

> "Go down to Keilah, for I am going to give the Philistines into your hand."
>
> 1 Samuel 23:4

So David and his men went to Keilah and fought like crazy, and when it was all said and done, they walked away with a victory, delivering the people of Keilah from a nasty foe. Sadly, when King Saul heard the news of David's victory in rescuing the inhabitants of Keilah, he jealously instructed his men to attack David and his followers. This sent David back to begging God for further direction. In a series of direction prayers, David gets the answers he needs.

> Now David knew that Saul was plotting evil against him; so he said to Abiathar the priest, "Bring the ephod here."
>
> Then David said, "O LORD God of Israel, Your servant has heard for certain that Saul is seeking to come to Keilah to destroy the city on my account. Will the men of Keilah surrender me into his hand? Will Saul come down just as Your servant has heard? O LORD God of Israel, I pray, tell Your servant." And the LORD said, "He will come down."
>
> Then David said, "Will the men of Keilah surrender me and my men into the hand of Saul?" And the LORD said, "They will surrender you."
>
> 1 Samuel 23:9 – 12 NASB

With no time for fluff or distraction, David asks, and the Lord speaks. The essence of direction prayer is that it needs a timely answer. The answer David received from God was the opposite of what was expected. After David and his men bravely faced danger in rescuing the people of Keilah, you would think the recipients of this good deed would at least cover for David when asked about his whereabouts. God said that wasn't going to happen, and fortunately David listened to his voice rather than to the voice of human reason.

Many people share with me that when they pray for direction, they need clear answers to circumstances that have grown to hurricane force. But they struggle to know how to listen for the way God responds. We can learn from the way David approached this type of prayer:

- David expected to get immediate answers to his timely questions.
- David didn't rationalize or talk himself out of the way he sensed that God was answering.
- David didn't consult all his boys. He didn't sit on it for days (that is a different type of prayer). He needed to hear and move — and he did.
- David didn't think himself into a tizzy! He prayed with deliberate focus as he asked for the ephod to be brought out. The ephod was a vest that symbolized the intentional act of prayer. It was a tool that helped those who prayed to lock in on what they were asking for. Simply looking at the ephod directed David's mind to a focus and belief that bolstered the importance of what he was asking.
- Hearing from God prompted movement. David *postured* himself to pray and then *positioned* himself to move.

Direction prayer launches from a specific need that requires immediate attention and response from God. Our part is to pray for direction as we wait expectantly for God to give a timely answer.

DEFINING PRAYER

A page in my Bible has been so loved, so cried on, so pored over that it literally has ripped in two. Yellowing tape holds it together, and the corner of the page has been turned so many times that it now has a jagged edge rather than smooth. This page is tucked in the fifth chapter of John, and it holds ramifications that I sometimes want to run from rather than embrace.[*]

A man who had been sick for thirty-eight years (most scholars think he was paralyzed, unable to walk) lay by a pool of water. This pool was a haven for struggling people. Those who were sick, blind,

---

[*] I tell this story briefly in my book *Truly Fed* (Kansas City, Mo.: Beacon Hill, 2009), 12.

lame, and withered gathered there to wait for a stirring of the waters. According to Jewish tradition, an angel of the Lord stirred the waters at certain seasons, and the first to enter the water after the stirring was healed of whatever afflicted them. Walking the streets of Jerusalem, Jesus saw this man lying on his mat, helpless and deformed. He then asked a question that seems utterly ridiculous.

> When Jesus saw him lying there, and *knew* that he had already been a long time in that condition, He said to him "Do you wish to get well?"
>
> John 5:6 NASB, emphasis mine

It is evident this man has had a life that makes the word *difficult* seem too soft. Lying on a dirty mat, hoping against hope that someone would feel sorry for you and toss you a coin — that was the best you could hope for. If Jesus already knew he had been lying there for a long time, why did he ask the probing question, "Do you wish to get well?" It seems almost rude to ask a crippled man if he wants to dance.

The man doesn't answer immediately. Actually, he doesn't answer at all, but immediately begins to rehearse his excuses.

> "Sir," the invalid replied, "I have no one to help me into the pool when the water is stirred. While I am trying to get in, someone else goes down ahead of me."
>
> John 5:7

Jesus calmly looks at him, and with the wisdom of a parent who sees beyond excuses, he boldly issues this command, with a startling outcome:

> "Get up! Pick up your mat and walk." At once the man was cured; he picked up his mat and walked.
>
> John 5:8 – 9

A man who had spent thirty-eight years on the ground now stood on the deformed limbs that once had been useless.

It strikes me that Jesus asks us this very question when we utter prayers from our dirty mats: "Do you really want to get well? Do you really want to do what it takes to see a change in your life?" I can honestly answer that at times in my life excuses have crowded out my ability to answer yes.

How can we pray for release from embarrassing habits, crushing attitudes, or overpowering gloom when we aren't prepared to face this probing question that slams into our wall of despair? Jesus asks, "Do you wish to get well?" because he wants us to clarify and define where we truly are in our lives and why we keep screaming out the same prayers without the slightest hope, belief, or confidence that change can take place.

First, Jesus instructs the man to *get up*. This is, of course, an impossible task for someone who has lived in the dirt for almost four decades, yet this is where Jesus starts. In defining prayer, it's as though Jesus uses the knife of a surgeon to cut through the flesh of our excuses and doubt. I wish he would use a butter knife and gently pat me with butter, but he doesn't.

We may pray such things as, "Restore my marriage, Lord," or "Heal my body," or "Keep my kids out of trouble" while Jesus is asking, "Do you really want to do what it takes to be well? Are you willing to humble yourself with your spouse and offer grace? Are you willing to let go of habits that abuse your health and body? Are you willing to stick with a cohesive plan that sets boundaries of safety for your children?"

The great thing about God is that his love for us isn't dependent on how well we behave for him. His love is bolstered by how he invites us to transform. He cuts through the froth of our words and stitches up the wounds of our hearts. While breakthrough prayer opens new doorways to walk through, defining prayer mobilizes the steps we take to walk through them. Defining prayer takes good intentions and turns them into changed behavior.

The second thing Jesus instructs this man to do is to *pick up his mat*. You can imagine how dirty this thing must have been. Lying on something for years can make it stink. Jesus tells him to pick it up. I'll never forget the comments of a woman I loved who struggled greatly in her life. She could not understand why Jesus would want us to take the mat with us. Why not just leave it on the ground and walk away?

I let her question simmer for a while before trying to address it. The next time we talked, I asked if maybe Jesus instructed the man to roll it up and take it with him as a reminder of where he had come from. Every time he looked at the mat or held it in his hands, maybe it pushed him to a point of praise as he remembered what it was like to crawl. When we experience transformation with God, it is liberating to give God bragging rights. Nothing does this better than remembering where we've come from.

The final instruction God gives this man is to *walk*. In other words, move on, respond to the healing I've given you. Don't just talk about it; don't just keep it to yourself. Move on it in a way that people can now see you're walking. Can you imagine what would have happened if Jesus had brought about healing in this man's life but he refused to get up and move from that spot? The man gained strength the more he moved. He walked, skipped, jumped, and ran, as he used legs that had been useless for so long. It may have taken a while to get his balance, but he moved — and he was never the same.

This Scripture has deep personal meaning for me as the daughter of a paralyzed man. After my dad's car accident, he lived in a wheelchair, possessing little movement in his hands and arms and no movement in his legs. I watched him clamp down on his arm brace with his teeth so he could hold a fork or grasp a comb. He waited in his hospital bed for a nurse to get him up in the morning, and he waited at night to be put to bed.

Toward the end of my father's life, his heart was giving out, and most of his bodily functions were failing. He spent the last few weeks of his life away from the small mountain hospital he lived in and in a

Denver hospital close to me, my sister, my brother, and my mom. We were so happy to have those weeks with him, whispering sweet stories to him and holding his hands as we visited.

Each day, the nurses would turn my dad, moving him into different positions so his bedsores wouldn't get worse. The thing about bedsores is that once you get them, they are extremely hard to get rid of, especially when you're paralyzed and don't have good circulation in parts of your body. One day, a young nurse came into my dad's room as I sat by his bedside. She literally gasped as she uncovered his legs. His limbs looked like those of a skeleton with a thin strip of skin over the bones. The skin that was there was covered in pussing sores — red, blue, and brown spots of rotting flesh. I was shocked but tried to maintain my composure as I realized that it had been years since I had seen the flesh of Dad's legs, uncovered from the protection of pants or bedsheets. I held his hands as the nurse shifted his position, and I thought about the absolute helplessness of not even being able to turn over on your side. A few short days later, my dad passed away, taking his last breath as my sister sat near him. I was shocked to realize that my dad had been in his paralyzed condition for exactly thirty-eight years. The precise number of years this man in the Bible had lived with mangled limbs.

Once in a while someone will ask me about my dad. What about his healing? Didn't he, too, want to get well? There was a time when my dad and I had this conversation. I was young and headstrong, feeling quite convinced that the sure sign of healing was only what could be seen physically. My dad felt otherwise. He explained that he had peace with God, and so he lived his life with quiet reserve from the seat of his wheelchair. Tethered to a chair, yet free with his God. But Jesus had different plans for this man with battered limbs who lay by the pool, and I know firsthand what those limbs must have looked like. Even now it makes me weep to think about it. When Jesus told him to get up and walk on legs that had been covered with sores and a thin layer of flesh on bone, it was nothing short of a transforming miracle. This man left the encounter walking.

This is what God invites us to in defining prayer. If we are willing to get up and move, he will transform us. From crawling to running, from hiding to basking in his glory, from lying on a filthy mat to tucking it under our arms and moving on.

chapter 8

—

THE TENSION OF BELIEF

*I*n some of my fondest childhood memories of my mom, she is always wearing the same thing — her fluffy bathrobe. Actually, it started out white and fluffy, and by the time I left for college, it was a faded matte mass of pinkish gray. She wore the same robe for thirteen years, and it wasn't just at bedtime. I remember us going out and about with her wearing that robe. We took trips to the grocery store, had conversations with neighbors, and ran in and out of the drugstore in a blur of pinkish-gray terry cloth! Mom worked full-time most of my life and always dressed to a tee, but on any given weekend that bathrobe was the wardrobe favorite.

Not too long ago it struck me that I've followed in her footsteps. I have slept in the same T-shirt for over twenty-one years. It's a shirt Bobby wore when he played for the Kansas City Royals. At the time our son, Colton, was an infant, and as he graduates from college this year, I feel like I am just now breaking this shirt in. The other day I woke up in it, went for a jog, came home, and spent my entire day in my pajama shirt running errands. A part of me chooses cozy over presentable, easy over effort. I love this shirt, but I'm always hoping I don't see anyone when I'm wearing it.

Sometimes I think we wear our belief in God like bathrobes or soft pajamas. Although we may be comfortable in our jammies, we are not functioning at our best in them. When it comes to faith, we have to get out of our bathrobes and believe.

But what does it mean to believe in something? What does it look like to have faith? How can I slip out of my robe of comfort and dress myself with belief?

The author of Hebrews writes, "Faith is the assurance of things hoped for, the conviction of things not seen" (Hebrews 11:1 NASB). I've spent the better part of my adulthood trying to wrap my brain around these weighty words. Every serious believer has, at some point or other, scratched her or his head trying to understand it.

Our Spirit hunger longs to engage God in prayer, but prayer walks hand in hand with belief, and this is the area where we can wander off the path into spiritual quicksand. We want to believe that what we pray for will transpire, but the quicksand pulls us down as soon as the prayers leave our hearts. This struggle — this grappling to believe — is what I call *holy tension.*

- I pray for a healthy marriage, but I don't think ours can be repaired.
- I pray to feel better, but I know it's hopeless.
- I pray for a new beginning, but I'm sure I'll just crawl back to my old habits.

Holy tension pulls and tugs at our belief, trying to take it under.

In Scripture, a picture of holy tension can be found in the life of a father whose faith and belief are slamming into one another.

A man in the crowd answered, "Teacher, I brought you my son, who is possessed by a spirit that has robbed him of speech. Whenever it seizes him, it throws him to the ground. He foams at the mouth, gnashing his teeth and becomes rigid. I asked your disciples to drive out the spirit, but they could not." ...

So they brought him. When the spirit saw Jesus, it immediately threw the boy into a convulsion. He fell to the ground and rolled around, foaming at the mouth.

Mark 9:17 – 18, 20

If you've ever witnessed someone having a seizure, you know how unsettling this can be. When Bobby and I started dating, he told me he was electrocuted when he was twelve years old. He and his cousin were playing a forbidden game of football in the living room when the ball accidentally crashed into the TV. Bobby picked up a metal letter opener and inserted it into an outlet on the TV that looked broken. He shot across the room flailing and seizing, much to the horror of his cousin Michael. From that day forward, he began to have regular seizures, never knowing when they would strike.

The first time I saw Bobby have a seizure, I thought he was going to die. We were in the hallway of our apartment complex in New York. He had flown all night with the Yankees and was up early to come with me to take our car in for servicing. As we walked down the dim hallway, I noticed he was beginning to shake, and then he dropped to the floor in a tangle of convulsions. I was banging on doors trying to get someone to help, but no one would answer, even though I could hear radios and the sound of people brushing their teeth.

When the convulsions stopped, I tried to drag Bobby's limp body down the hallway and into our apartment. I dialed 911 and waited. He was unresponsive, and I remembered how he had instructed me *not* to call 911. Our sports agent didn't want people to know that Bobby had trouble with seizures because he was afraid his value as a player might diminish. But every time I saw him have a seizure, I did the same thing — dialed 911. This kind of experience is too scary to face by yourself, and I welcomed the sound of the paramedics' footsteps coming to help.

This father in Scripture had no paramedics to call. Little did he know he was in the presence of *the* paramedic. As the boy rolled on the ground and foamed at the mouth, Jesus stopped to ask the father a question. Personally, if I had been in the crowd, I might have shouted, "Talk to him later. Just heal the boy already!" Jesus was in no hurry. He wanted to let the father fully explain his pain.

> And He asked his father, "How long has this been happening to him?" And he said, "From childhood. It has often thrown him both into the fire and into the water to destroy him. But if You can do anything, take pity on us and help us!"
>
> And Jesus said to him, " 'If You can?' All things are possible to him who believes."
>
> Immediately the boy's father cried out and said, "*I do believe; help my unbelief.*"
>
> Mark 9:21 – 24 NASB, emphasis mine

Oh, how I love this father. In the same breath he utters, "I do believe — but help me because I don't believe!" Listening to him is utterly confusing and messy. It's like listening to something any of us would cry if what we loved more than life was writhing on the ground.

Jesus speaks sanity into the situation as a crowd of curious bystanders gathers to gawk.

> When Jesus saw that a crowd was rapidly gathering, He rebuked the unclean spirit, saying to it, "You deaf and mute spirit, I command you, come out of him and do not enter him again."
>
> After crying out and throwing him into terrible convulsions, it came out; and the boy became so much like a corpse that most of them said, "He is dead!"
>
> *But Jesus* took him by the hand and raised him; and he got up.
>
> Mark 9:25 – 27 NASB, emphasis mine

Often people wonder, "Is it possible for things to get worse after you've prayed about them?" You bet it is. Jesus spoke life and truth over this boy's life, and he plummeted into a seizure so terrible that it had everyone gasping, "He's dead!"

I bet they were smugly whispering that the boy's dad would have been better off if he hadn't even bothered coming to Jesus for help. At least his boy would still be alive.

Just when it couldn't get any worse, two of the most powerful words in Scripture leap off the page and change the entire script: *But Jesus.* Whenever we see these two words placed next to each other, miracles follow.

But Jesus means that although our lives may look dead, he is raising them up.

But Jesus means that in spite of the hushed whispers or gasps of those who don't understand, we trust a Savior who heals our souls.

But Jesus means that even though we struggle to believe in him, he steadily believes in us.

If only we would wait for our "but Jesus" instead of taking our cues from a negative crowd, we might well be able to grapple more gracefully with the holy tension of belief.

What Causes Holy Tension?

The causes of holy tension are both subtle and stark. They're evident and yet sneaky. I believe this tension thrives from four sources: doubt, fear, embarrassment, and spiritual scar tissue. Each of these tensions has the ability to snuff out faith.

Doubt

When I was a new believer, I used to go into a panic whenever I felt a shred of doubt because I knew that somewhere in the Bible, doubt was considered bad.

If any of you lacks wisdom, you should ask God, who gives generously to all without finding fault, and it will be given to you. But when you ask, you must believe and not doubt, because the one who doubts is like a wave of the sea, blown and tossed by the wind. That person should not expect to receive anything from the Lord. Such a person is double-minded and unstable in all they do.

James 1:5 – 8

These words are enough to leave anyone who reads them with a stomachache. I was sickened by the feeling that I can't expect anything if I doubt. Who believes perfectly? Is there any lover of God who doesn't sometimes doubt?

The *Life Application Bible* notes that James, Jesus' brother, "wrote to Jewish Christians who had been scattered throughout the Mediterranean world because of persecution. In their hostile surroundings they were tempted to let intellectual agreement pass for true faith."[10] Sadly, when it comes to intellectual agreement, we may be agreeing with something that leads us straight into a dump. James is trying to smack this thinking upside the head — to expose the futility of "What's the point of saying you love God but then contradicting the gospel with your life?" As I floundered, trying to make sure I wasn't *that* kind of believer, I read these words in the *Life Application Bible*, which fleshed out this concept clearly:

What is a doubtful mind? It is a mind that is not completely convinced that God's way is best. It treats God's Word like any human advice, retaining the option for disobedience. It vacillates between feelings, the world's ideas, and God's commands. The cure for a doubtful mind is wholehearted commitment to God's reliable way."[11]

In the context of this definition, if we are fully convinced that God is God — and believe that his word is authority and his commands are nourishment — then we are not double-minded.

I sometimes shake my head when I see something written in a magazine about faith in God and then see a horoscope in a column right next to it. Or when I hear the name of Jesus lumped next to Buddha's. Belief in God isn't like decorating cupcakes — a sprinkle of this and a sprinkle of that. Real belief in God doesn't make up its own rules of engagement; these guidelines are already designed and written in the most sacred of invitations, the Bible. Why I've wasted time with other invitations is now beyond my ability to comprehend.

So if you are in love with God, are truly born into a life with him, and refuse to choose a sinful life as a two-faced believer, you aren't double-minded if you have doubts; you are human.

I've come to realize that doubt can actually serve a good purpose if we let it. I call this "productive doubt," and nobody illustrates this better than Peter.

It had been a rough period for Jesus and the disciples. Jesus had received news that his relative and friend John the Baptist had been murdered by a slandering king. Jesus withdrew to a lonely place by boat, but when the multitudes heard this, they swarmed out of the cities to find him. When he rowed ashore, thousands of people were waiting for him. After a full day of healing bodies, Jesus fed souls as he increased a meager five loaves and two fish to a meal that would supply multitudes. After the masses were fed, Jesus instructed his disciples to get into the boat and to go ahead of him to the other side. It's stunning how Jesus is always thinking of other people. You'd think *he* would have escaped on the boat and let his disciples disperse the crowds, but he chose the reverse.

After everyone was gone, Jesus went up the mountain alone to pray. While he was praying, the disciples were panicking out on the sea with weather gone bad. Their craft was many miles away from shore, battered like a toy boat in a waterfall. The hills surrounding the Sea of Galilee act like a wind tunnel, and waves as high as ten feet could quickly overpower a wooden fishing boat.

Sometime between the hours of 3:00 and 6:00 a.m. these terrified men saw a sight that was even more mind-bending; they saw Jesus walking on the waves. Since the storm began in the evening, it was possible they had been rocked by dark waves for close to nine hours before they saw Jesus. They probably thought their minds were playing tricks on them, prompting a response both amusing and human.

> When the disciples saw Him walking on the sea, they were terrified, and said, "It is a ghost!" And they cried out in fear.
> But immediately Jesus spoke to them, saying, "Take courage, it is I; do not be afraid."
>
> Matthew 14:26 – 27 NASB

Something welled up in Peter. Maybe it was that fresh memory of just having seen Jesus feed multitudes, or maybe he was so sick of the terror in the boat that a surge of testosterone overcame him, but something snapped and caused him to cry out.

> Peter said to Him, "Lord, if it is You, command me to come to You on the water."
>
> Matthew 14:28 NASB

I can just see the other disciples holding on to his robe to try to keep him in the boat! But in that blast of bold faith, there was no stopping him. Jesus calmly responded, "Come" — and Peter climbed out of the boat into the raging sea.

> Then Peter got down out of the boat, walked on the water and came toward Jesus. But when he saw the wind, he was afraid and, beginning to sink, cried out, "Lord, save me!"
>
> Matthew 14:29 – 30

Whether Peter took his eyes off Jesus for a moment and looked at how the wind was roaring around him or a wave came up and blocked his sight of the One he was walking toward, suddenly his brave faith turned to doubt.

It's interesting that Peter usually gets a bad rap for this scene. Preachers often ask, "Why didn't Peter have more faith? Why did he doubt?" Well, now, I don't see any other disciple putting a toe on that water! Not only do I respect his courage, but what Peter did in the midst of doubt is nothing short of brilliant. He screamed out, "Lord, save me!" and in an instant the whole picture changed. In the midst of troubling circumstances, we can learn as much from what we don't do as from what we do. Peter didn't try to fight the waves himself. He realized he was utterly helpless in the violent storm and recognized his need to cry out. He didn't ignore the fact that he was sinking, and he didn't scramble back into the boat for dear life.

In the midst of storms, *who we cry to* and *what we cry* make all the difference. "Lord, save me!" is one of the most audacious prayers ever uttered. It ushers in the power and breath of the living God.

Immediately Jesus reached out his hand and caught him. "You of little faith," he said, "why did you doubt?"

And when they climbed into the boat, the wind died down. Then those who were in the boat worshiped him, saying, "Truly you are the Son of God."

Matthew 14:31 – 33

Most people picture Jesus saying, "Why did you doubt?" with a sense of disappointment, but I think he said it with a look of pride. I can just picture Jesus pushing the wet hair out of Peter's eyes and smiling as if to say, "You really are something, Peter! I'm proud of you."

It's fascinating to watch the effect belief has on those who stand by and watch. The other disciples, who remained in the boat, had to be holding their breath as Peter climbed out onto the stormy sea. Then, in the midst of the spitting waves, they watched him sink. But in an instant, Jesus had Peter in his arms; Jesus crouched in the boat with them, and the storm was over. This hails one of my favorite words in the Bible — *worship*.

Worship transcends fear. Worship transcends doubt. Really, *all* of the disciples experienced doubt that stormy night. But doubt isn't the point when it comes to matters of belief; getting out of the boat is. The experience of doubt doesn't have to be crippling, as long as we keep getting out of our boats and remembering just who it is we look at.

Fear

Another cause of holy tension is fear. I take comfort in the fact that every single person I admire in the Bible struggled with fear. No exceptions. One person I thought might be exempt is the apostle Paul. Like a polished public speaker, he always seemed to know what to say and how to say it. But in a couple of brief verses in the book of Acts we see a hint of fear in Paul so forceful that Jesus himself showed up to deal with it.

> And the Lord said to Paul in the night by a vision, "Do not be afraid any longer, but go on speaking and do not be silent; for I am with you, and no man will attack you in order to harm you, for I have many people in this city."
>
> Acts 18:9 – 10 NASB

Why does the dark of night seem to magnify fear? It is typically in the night watches that my breath grows short as my mind rehearses the script of anxiety. I've often wondered what Paul was afraid of that night. Was it speaking to people who opposed his message? He seemed to have come through that with flying colors many times before. Was it being imprisoned for his words and faith? Been there and done that too. As Paul had lain on that bed in the city of Corinth, drenched in fear, Jesus showed up and spoke one sentence that rearranged Paul's mind.

Some time after leaving Corinth after this night of fear, Paul wrote a letter that magnified the things that caused his fear. It was a list of pain and terror, joy and confidence, that swung back and forth like a lively game of Ping-Pong.

> In everything commending ourselves as servants of God, in much endurance, in afflictions, in hardships, in distresses, in beatings, in imprisonments, in tumults, in labors, in sleeplessness, in hunger, in purity, in knowledge, in patience, in kindness, in the Holy Spirit, in genuine love, in the word of truth, in the power of God; by the weapons of righteousness for the right hand and the left, by glory and dishonor, by evil report and good report, regarded as deceivers and yet true; as unknown and yet well-known, as dying yet behold, we live; as punished yet not put to death, as sorrowful yet always rejoicing, as poor yet making many rich, as having nothing yet possessing all things.
>
> 2 Corinthians 6:4 – 10 NASB

It's shocking to realize that Paul stuffed all these fears into one long thought! Every emotion imaginable is captured in this exquisite run-on sentence. Are we struggling with hardships, afflictions, sleeplessness, bondage, a prison of some kind, people bad-mouthing us, financial troubles, physical abuse? We're in good company, because so did Paul.

Interestingly, he also struggled with a type of fear that seems to trample hope. The fear of gloomy depression.

> For even when we came into Macedonia our flesh had no rest, but we were afflicted on every side: conflicts without, fears within. But God, who comforts the depressed, comforted us by the coming of Titus.
>
> 2 Corinthians 7:5 – 6 NASB

Paul, a lighthouse to everyone he meets, struggled with the same fears we do. He even understood the despair of depression and thanked God for sending someone like Titus to comfort him. But I'm still left wondering how Paul changed his thinking. How did he fight the kind of fear that plays out in our heads long before it shows up in our actions? Later in that same letter to the Corinthians, he explains.

> For though we walk in the flesh, we do not war according to the flesh, for the weapons of our warfare are not of the flesh, but divinely powerful for the destruction of fortresses. We are destroying speculations and every lofty thing raised up against the knowledge of God, and we are taking every thought captive to the obedience of Christ.
>
> 2 Corinthians 10:3 – 5 NASB

I call this the "fear punch" because it knocks fear out of the ring with two blows to the gut. Bobby has explained to me that boxers try to hit their opponents with a two-blow punch. The first blow stuns; the second blow crushes. Paul explains that our weapons for dealing with fear are mental. First, we offer the *stun punch* by destroying lofty things raised up against the knowledge of God. Truthfully, isn't this all that fear is? Thinking about things as if they are greater than God is? Bills, health, relationships, uncertainty, and the like can all start to look pretty lofty in comparison to God when fear has on the boxing gloves. But Paul reminds us to stun this opponent by remembering God.

Paul then offers the *crush punch* as he instructs us to take thoughts captive to the obedience of Christ. To take something captive is to hold it down and make it obey. Our thoughts are like an unruly toddler who secretly desires some discipline. If we don't discipline our thoughts and make them obey Jesus, they'll find something destructive, bland, or fearful to obey.

Every time I use the metal strainer in my kitchen, it reminds me of what we need to do with our thoughts. After we cook pasta, we take the softened noodles that have been boiled and pour them into the strainer, while the glue-like water they were boiled in slides down the drain. We would never slap the gluey water *and* the noodles onto a plate and pour a rich, tomatoey sauce on top. That would be disgusting, but that's what our thought life often reflects. I like to think of our mental strainer as a thought filter. We choose what stays and what goes down the drain. The noodles, the good stuff, are what we want to keep. If our thoughts don't line up with *peace* (Philippians 4:7), *freedom* (John 8:31 – 32), *hope* (Romans 15:13), and *purpose* (Philippians 2:13), they need to go down the drain, because they're not lining up with God's voice in our lives.[12]

We get to choose what we allow to grow and fester in our heads. We get to pick what stays and what has to go. We're pulling down fortresses one fear at a time.

Embarrassment

As a teacher, I've seen embarrassment rob more kids of growth than any other factor. They make many decisions based on avoiding embarrassment rather than promoting learning. The truth is that we all protect ourselves from being embarrassed, sometimes at the risk of excavating a fresh nugget from God.

Why don't we believe God for more in our lives? What makes us ignore our Spirit hunger and sink into disbelief? Could it be that sometimes we're embarrassed by what others might think of *our* faith, and other times we're embarrassed when other people move out in *their* faith?

I'll never forget my first Bible study leader at San Diego State University. Each week, this feisty college student would lead a group through the pages of the Gospels. I thought he was nothing short of Billy Graham. When I found out he was a huge fan of our college baseball team, my spirits soared as I realized I could return some of the blessing by introducing him to my boyfriend, the team's star shortstop.

On the day of our planned meeting, I met him in the parking lot behind the baseball stadium. He had on a T-shirt that read "Jesus is Lord," which secretly thrilled me because I had been trying to explain my newfound love for Jesus to my boyfriend, Bobby, but didn't seem to be making any headway. Somewhere deep inside of me, I thought that if

Bobby could just see how much this guy loved the Lord — he was wearing a T-shirt with "Jesus is Lord" on it, for goodness' sake! — he would want Jesus in his life too.

As we approached the field, I noticed that my friend was making some strange body movements. The closer we got to the dugout and the players, the more he covered up the writing on his shirt with his forearms. By the time I introduced him to Bobby, he was acting kind of mousy and obviously embarrassed by the shirt I was so proud of.

Feeling devastated, I wondered what happened to the bold Bible study leader I knew. In the company of ballplayers, he shrunk into an embarrassed heap of stutters and cover-up. It didn't take me long as a new believer to realize that often my intent doesn't match my action. Sometimes we let the creepy fear of embarrassment choke out the confidence of faith.

A couple of years ago, I received some unlikely tutoring on this topic. A group of women had been meeting in my bedroom to pray. We called ourselves the "Upper Room Prayer Women," and we always met at night, with soft candles burning and spa music gently massaging our spirits as we engaged God with our requests.

One night as we finished, a woman named Jamie said she had something to share about the last time we had met. She was about seven months pregnant with her second child, glowing from head to toe as she spoke. "I have to tell you something that's embarrassing, but I know the Lord wants me to share it," she explained. We encouraged her to go on. "When we were praying last week, I felt like the Lord was nudging me to pray for Angelina Jolie." We all giggled at this point, wondering why in the world God would nudge her to pray for a star none of us personally knew. Angelina was pregnant with twins at the time and quite regularly in the news, but to pray for her seemed to border on the ridiculous. "It seemed stupid to me, and I was too embarrassed to pray for her in front of you all. When I got in the car, I couldn't shake the feeling that I had let God down by not praying. Then I heard a message in my heart so clear that it almost knocked me over," she said. "God showed me that it wasn't the actual praying for Angelina Jolie that was important, but the obedience to pray, even if I was embarrassed."

From that day on, we vowed to pray for anything we felt led to pray for, even if it seemed embarrassing or ridiculous. If Brad Pitt receives a drenching cover in prayer, you'll know where it's coming from.

When we let the derogatory opinions or scornful stares of others define our faith, we shrink back into a shriveled heap. Our love relationship with the Lord doesn't dim, but embarrassment can steal some amazing moments — moments that are meant for sweet glory.

The second type of embarrassment is displayed in the believer who is embarrassed when others try to live out *their* faith. I can't tell you how many times I've been advised, "Maybe faith should remain private. Why speak so openly about your faith?" These voices echo as the uncomfortable sighs of embarrassment seek to derail my belief. What good is believing in something if you can't share its potent outcome?

I was thrilled to find the story of an outcast in Scripture who wasn't embarrassed by his faith. He had a lot of strikes against him. He was a beggar, so no one paid much attention to him, other than to be annoyed by him; he was a seemingly inconsequential speck of humanity in a multitude of people; and he was blind.

Jesus was on his way to Jerusalem where for a brief moment in his ministry he was treated like a rock star. People were following him with fervor, and there was a certain vibe to the crowd as they marched along the road in a parade of delight over this celebrity with whom they were infatuated. But there on the side of the road was a poor, blind beggar named Bartimaeus, who had taken to shouting Jesus' name at the top of his lungs. "Jesus, Son of David, have mercy on me!" (Mark 10:47).

Over and over he screamed, unable to see the looks of disgust and disdain people were inflicting on him. Aware that this beggar was messing with the festive mood of the crowd, many people tried to silence him as they screamed at him to be quiet. But he didn't care. He screamed out even louder.

"Son of David, have mercy on me!"

Jesus stopped and said, "Call him."

So they called to the blind man, "Cheer up! On your feet! He's calling you."

Mark 10:48 – 49

How ironic that the very crowd that was pushing him aside and telling him to shush up now circles around him in delight, saying, "Hey you, good news! Jesus wants to talk to you!"

This reminds me of the fan mentality I often see in pro ball. I remember sitting at a Yankee spring training game with my mother-in-law while zealous fans behind us were screaming a string of less than flattering words about my husband. I was accustomed to this kind of thing, but I sensed that my mother-in-law's blood pressure was rising. Before I could muzzle her, she let loose with a few precise tidbits for those fans that set them straight. She told them how he had played most of the previous season with a tendon flapping in his wrist because he didn't want to let down the team. She spelled out statistics that even I didn't know about my husband, and finally she screamed, "*And* he's my son!"

You would have thought my husband was a Hall of Fame player after that. They were gushing and oozing compliments about every ball he hit. It was fake and silly, but did I ever see a clear picture of the mentality of those who follow something because it's thrilling rather than because they are understanding its truth.

Out of all the adoring shouts and screams Jesus heard that day, he chose to single out the cries of a blind beggar.

Throwing his cloak aside, he jumped to his feet and came to Jesus.

"What do you want me to do for you?" Jesus asked him.

The blind man said, "Rabbi, I want to see."

"Go," said Jesus, "your faith has healed you." Immediately he received his sight and followed Jesus along the road.

Mark 10:50 – 52

I would love to have heard the conversations surrounding clear-eyed Bartimaeus, a former sightless "throwaway" in the crowd's eyes, now a part of the throng walking with the Master. We have much to learn from this man and his screams. He didn't let other people's embarrassment squelch his need for Jesus. Oh, may we keep screaming our need for mercy at the top of our lungs, even if everyone around us is telling us to hush.

Spiritual Scar Tissue

A final reason we find ourselves stuck in holy tension rather than belief is spiritual scar tissue. When we've been wounded — I mean really hurt, abused, bashed, run over, betrayed — this produces scar tissue. Even after walking through steps of forgiveness and healing, there is emotional and spiritual evidence that our spirit has endured a blow.

One of the scars in my life is the pain of infidelity. Although my husband and I allowed the Lord to cleanse this infected wound with an antiseptic strong enough to bring about new life, every now and then I am reminded that I have a scar. The reminder can come as I sit inside a movie theater, watching people laugh at adultery as if it's no big deal; as I watch ballplayers sneak out at night when their darling wives and babies are at home missing them; or as I drive along and out of nowhere a memory of darkness smashes against me, causing me to cling to the truth that I know is real. Scar tissue heals, but doctors say it never heals exactly the same. In God's kingdom this can be a good thing, because he tends to heal the tissue of scars more profoundly than before, making a scar useful instead of just ugly.

I've talked to countless women who have been wounded and scarred — left to raise kids alone after a searing divorce, abused by words or physical actions too shameful to bear, neglected and forgotten as if they're invisible. Scars have a funny way of trying to become the center of attention. But part of believing God is to grow in understanding that a scar from our past does not define the new flesh of our future. God wants to do fascinating, adventurous things in our lives; we don't want to be left behind, still picking at our scars.

I've learned a lot from the spiritual scar tissue in my marriage. I don't pick at the scar and try to make it bleed. Many times after we've shouldered great pain, it's tempting to keep scratching at that scar until it reopens and gushes a fresh stream of blood. The apostle Paul shares that if anyone is in Christ, "the new creation has come: The old has gone, the new is here!" (2 Corinthians 5:17).

I've often used this verse as both ointment and escape. How do I reconcile the pain that resurfaces without getting lost in the scar tissue? The essence of forgiveness is not that we forget the pain but that it doesn't define or dictate who we are.

Many women wear their scars like a piece of clothing. The first thing they show you after you meet them is their scar. "See it! See it!" they proclaim, as if it's the only part of them available for viewing. "How can I believe in God when I've got this scar that proves he doesn't care?"

God doesn't cause scars; humanity and sin do. But what if he could turn our scars into healed tissue that functions better than before? What if he could take a scar in our life and offer healing for the wounded tissue in another's life? We're worth so much more than our scars!

Each summer, my grandparents would take us to the lively beach town of Ocean City, Maryland — a place they trekked to every summer following their honeymoon. To this day, it's one of my favorite spots on earth. My grandmother would speak in her Southern drawl as she pulled a small package from her beach bag. Every summer it was the same lecture: "Gar-a-lyn [combining my first and middle name into a garbled woo that held its syllable for a long breath], the best thing in the world for scars is cocoa butter. Put a little of this over your arms and legs."

I can still smell that cocoa butter, fresh and healing, mixed with the fragrance of coconut and suntan lotion. I have no idea if it ever improved a scar on my skin, but my heart believed her completely. Today I have grown to realize that God is a God of cocoa butter, able to spread his healing balm over our bodies and minds, with the fresh scent of forgiveness and freedom, hope and inspiration, wafting in the air. What formerly held our belief hostage now glistens as tissue restored. Like the scars on the hands and feet of Jesus, my scars remind me of a gift — the gift of unwavering belief in spite of pain, gentle healing in spite of wounds.

THE HOLY TENSION OF WORDS

Holy tension plays out internally with doubt, fear, embarrassment, and scars. But it also plays out verbally with our words. When it comes to holy tension, what we say can affect what we believe.

Jesus was walking along with his disciples one morning and became hungry. He saw a fig tree full of green leaves by the side of the road. But when he reached out to pick a fig from the tree, he realized that though the tree looked good from a distance, it had no fruit on its limbs. He spoke directly to the tree: "May you never bear fruit again!" The Bible then describes what happened: "Immediately the tree withered" (Matthew 21:19).

I read this Scripture passage for a decade before I started to understand it. "Why take your frustration out on a tree?" I wondered. It seems a little like picking on a fern. As I've grown, I see the thread of teaching Jesus was trying to deliver through this scolded tree. The obvious moral is this: Just because something looks good from a distance doesn't mean there's anything real to it. We see this play out all the time in churches. People say they're lovers of Christ, yet they treat their dogs better than they treat people. They take God's Word, and while nodding at it, they live as if spitting on it as they hang out in the dark recesses of destructive habits and addiction rather than in freedom and light. I know because I was a tree like this — making sure to grow just the right color of leaves, never mind if there's no fruit to be picked.

But I think there is a deeper layer of teaching that Jesus slid in the backdoor that day as he taught his disciples. I believe he was trying to show them that faith works two ways. We can have positive faith or negative faith. Often, we have great amounts of negative faith in things we want changed for the positive.

I'm reminded of a childhood friend who grew up with a mom who was about as friendly as a hornet. Every time you were around her you felt you had just gotten stung. She was constantly telling my friend how clumsy she was. The truth is that my friend wasn't clumsy at all; she was actually quite graceful. But guess what she became every time we were around her mom — clumsy!

Jesus was showing his disciples that what we walk around cursing matters. He then launched into the most profound description of faith's power ever uttered.

> "Truly I tell you, if you have faith and do not doubt, not only can you do what was done to the fig tree, but also you can say to this mountain, 'Go, throw yourself into the sea,' and it will be done. If you believe, you will receive whatever you ask for in prayer."
>
> Matthew 21:21 – 22

I've always been a drama queen, and when I fell in love with Jesus, I fell hard. Living in the foothills of Colorado, I often put my Bible in a backpack and rode my bike to the base of the steep Rocky Mountains. I would stand there, and as if leading a cheer at a football game, I'd chant, "Move, mountain, move!" I would wait a few minutes and then start the chant again.

Never once did a mountain move. But one day the Lord whispered to my heart, "I'm talking about the mountains in your life! Bitterness, fear, insecurity, compulsivity ..."

"Oh, those mountains?" I sheepishly replied. "Yes, Lord, let's move them."

To tell you the truth, when someone believes Jesus can move a mountain out of her life, it's just as impressive as a literal mountain being uprooted from one place and moving to another.

Jesus was teaching the disciples that faith is a force to be reckoned with. He essentially said, "With the fig tree I had faith for a negative outcome; imagine what you can do with faith for a positive outcome!"

There's a reason Jesus says that cursing leads to withering. Who can stand under the weight of negative faith without shriveling? But on the other side of the mountain echoes an invitation bellowing out to us to believe. To say to our mountains, "Move!" and not budge until they do. To look unbelief squarely in the face and say, "Get out!"

Instead of walking around mountains or setting up tents and camping on them, we speak directly to them, as Jesus instructs us to do. Oswald Chambers wisely states, "God does not give us overcoming life; he gives us life as we overcome."[13] And it is with belief that we overcome our faith's greatest challenges.

PART THREE

a heart that moves

chapter 9

—

INVITED TO LISTEN

n order to receive a teaching certificate, you have to participate in the time-honored tradition of student teaching. The college I attended required that applicants complete two semesters of student teaching. When I was assigned to a class of first graders my first semester, I was silently giddy. "They'll be so much easier than the older kids," I thought. "Piece of cake!"

Little did I know that I was about to become the cake these cherubs devoured without the pretty icing. Each day I floundered through fabulously prepared lessons that no one listened to.

One day, a small boy named Woodrow seemed to sum up my first few weeks at this school. He was a tiny child with skin the color of an Oreo cookie and eyes and teeth as white as its filling. At the end of the day, I walked the class over to the busing area, and as Woodrow climbed the stairs of the bus, I thought I'd offer him an extra dose of my oozing kindness. Of all the first graders he was the toughest. He didn't listen and didn't participate, and like a pied piper, seemed to lead the other kids down a path of confused indifference. I truly thought I could win him over if I just saturated his hard exterior with sticky sweetness.

"Have a wonderful night, Woodrow," I gushed. "I can't wait to see you in class tomorrow, sweetie!" He looked at me with the intensity of a stun gun and shot back, "Shut up, stupid!" I about fell over backward. I didn't know whether to laugh or cry as I watched the bus slowly crawl away. I realized that Woodrow's words communicated what my mind instinctively knew but didn't want to admit: these kids didn't listen to me, nor did they respect me.

I went home that night and decided there needed to be a new sheriff in town. No more Mrs. Lollipop! I needed to get Woodrow and this class of tough six-year-olds roped in. The problem was that even the supervising teacher didn't seem to have much command in the room. It struck me that although we begged these kids daily to listen, they had no idea what good listening looked like. Resolutely I set out to teach them the body language of listening — how their eyes look when they're listening, how their mouths look (shut!) when they try to hear, and how even the posture of their bodies is a reflection of what they can absorb.

I wonder if God feels the same way. We pray and pour out petitions, but when it comes time to listen, it seems we really don't know how.

Spiritual listening has a body language of its own. It has its own physical and internal cues that prompt acceptance or rejection of what we're trying to absorb. In our quest to hear, it seems we encounter distinct listening types that demonstrate how "hard of hearing" we can be.

The eye-rolling listener: This type of listener already has her eyes rolled to the back of her head before you can finish encouraging her. She may not say anything, but her rolled eyes and cocked head say it all. "OK, that may work for *you*, but God never does things like that in *my* life!" With the stinging edge of sarcasm, the eye roller smashes any attempt at faith like a finger in a car door.

The Eeyore listener: One of my daughters was a Winnie the Pooh lover. Her entire room was decorated in Pooh and Piglet, Tigger and Eeyore. Bobby would often tease her when she'd get cranky by doing a spot-on Eeyore imitation. "Thanks for noticing me," the gray donkey would whine in a drone that was unnerving and predictable. "I guess I'll pray ... probably won't do any good ... but I suppose I should." Negative and gloomy, this type of listener drowns out with a nagging grayish slur anything they might hear.

The "there's something more important going on" listener: I worked for a boss several years ago who had the irritating habit of looking anywhere but in my eyes when I was trying to talk to her. As if at a gala event, her eyes would search out something or someone, looking over my shoulder and ignoring what was on my mind. I always walked away feeling as if what I had to say didn't really matter.

The constant chatter listener: Have you ever tried to hold a conversation with a cricket? The chirping vibrates through the air with an annoying rhythm that begs the question, "Do they ever stop for air?" I've been known to talk to God like this. Even if I let him get a word in edge-wise, it's loudly covered by a cycle of chirps so overbearing that an amplified megaphone couldn't break in.

It's often in these listening languages that I notice women lament, "I just don't hear from God!" Yet how we listen *for* God can determine our filling *by* him. So many of us beg to hear from God, and sadly, when he tries to speak, we bustle right by him.

POSTURES FOR HEARING FROM GOD

If listening has its own body language, then there's no better way to understand this dialect than by studying the postures that promote an attentive ear. Our hearts hold internal attitudes conducive to hearing from God, while our bodies settle into physical positions that help us hear. Our capacity to listen is like a child learning to walk. Certain postures must be present if a toddler is to remain upright. Hearing from God also requires postures that help us take our next steps: a humbling posture, a reviving posture, and an expectant posture.

The Humbling Posture: Posturing to Deflect the Focus from Ourselves

To be able to listen to God, we can't have pride intruding on the conversation. Pride is an unwelcome trespasser when we posture ourselves to listen. It will always try to shift God's whispers toward a different focus. Most often, that focus is me.

- **God whispers:** "Seek out the woman you saw last night. Give her a call; she's lonely."
- **Pride whispers:** "She ignored me. I'm not reaching out to someone who doesn't acknowledge how sweet I am!"
- **God whispers:** "Give your husband some grace. I'm weaving some valuable principles into his life, and he is weary."
- **Pride whispers:** "I don't deserve to be treated this way. If he doesn't shape up, then I don't have to!"

God directs, and pride deflects. Pride always tries to make *us* the point, while God makes *love* the point. The trouble is, we love being the point and will typically push out of the way anything that rivals our mirrored reflection.

Jesus illustrates this with precision as he exposes the listening postures of two unlikely men who go to the temple to pray. One man is a Pharisee, the religious equivalent of a church leader who craves the attention. The other is a low-life tax collector who lived a life of cheating and abuse.

"Two men went up into the temple to pray, one a Pharisee and the other a tax collector. The Pharisee stood and was praying this to *himself*: 'God, I thank You that I am not like other people: swindlers, unjust, adulterers, or even like this tax collector. I fast twice a week; I pay tithes of all that I get.'

"But the tax collector, standing some distance away, was even unwilling to lift up his eyes to heaven, but was beating his breast, saying, 'God, be merciful to me, the sinner!'

"I tell you, this man went to his house justified rather than the other; for everyone who exalts himself will be humbled, but he who humbles himself will be exalted."

Luke 18:10 – 14 NASB, emphasis mine

When I first started to digest these words of Jesus many years ago, I remember thinking, "God, thank you that I don't pray like the Pharisee did." All of a sudden, a slap of truth hit my face as I realized that I sounded just like him!

It's interesting to note that the Pharisee is really praying to *himself* and not to God. How different prayers sound when they have the hollow echo of promoting our own glory. The Pharisee notes that he is better than the swindlers and cheaters, never realizing that his very posture is prayer adultery.

Although it is easy to point fingers at robe-wearing religious men, I'm struck by how *our* prayer adultery sounds:

- Thanks for making me better than those people from the other side of the border.
- Thanks for making me better than those who have opposing political beliefs.
- Thanks for making me an effective parent, unlike some moms who can't control their kids.
- Thanks for making me lovable while many people are just tolerable.

Like the Pharisee, we mentally list the people we are superior to, and it doesn't stop there. After the "thankful I'm not like them" roll call, the Pharisee then spouts his spiritual résumé, sharing the sparkling things he does for God.

On the other side of the temple, Jesus notes the posture of the tax collector. This man recognizes his spiritual status and speaks with humility toward God. Unwilling to look toward heaven, he beats his chest and asks for mercy, not in a self-torturing way, but in a way that recognizes that God is perfect and he is not.

Jesus says if you exalt yourself (brag about yourself; push yourself to the forefront; shine the spotlight on yourself), you'll end up humbled, but if you humble yourself, you'll be exalted. He's *not* saying that both men aren't loved. He's just teaching that you're going to get humbled, one way or another, so why not adopt that posture from the start? The Bible states, "God is opposed to the proud, but gives grace to the humble. Therefore humble yourselves under the mighty hand of God, that He may exalt you *at the proper time*" (1 Peter 5:5 – 6 NASB, emphasis mine).

I remember when I figured out how to humble myself instead of waiting to be humbled. I thought our transition to the minor-league coaching scene would be easy. The Kansas City Royals offered us a job managing their short season — a team that in baseball hierarchy was pretty low. We were thrilled to get the job, and so we packed our three small children in the van and drove to Eugene, Oregon. When we got there, we were told they would put us up in a hotel until we could find an apartment to live in. I wasn't expecting the Ritz, but they put our entire family of five in a tiny room — cigarette burns on the lamps, a noisy highway next to our heads. To make matters worse, we had a tough time finding an apartment that would offer a short summer lease. We looked all over Eugene and finally settled on a rundown apartment complex that was definitely not in the Apartment Finders Guide. I had more than my share of prideful moments as I recalled our time with the Yankees and our nice home in New York — and now here we were in a place that boasted "Parking Space Included" as a bonus, when to all appearances most of the tenants could barely afford a car.

Shortly after we moved in, we celebrated our daughter Brooke's fifth birthday. She was a party girl at heart, and she wanted nothing more than a huge gathering of kids around a "My Little Pony" cake she had begged me to bake. In reality, we didn't know anyone in that town, let alone any kids. I knew her heart would break if we didn't have a party, so I prayed that God would show me what to do. "Humble yourself, Gari," I kept hearing. So with our baby son, Colton, in my arms and Brooke and Ally at my side, we knocked on every door of our apartment complex. Brooke had made dozens of homemade invitations and gleefully handed them to every person who opened the door.

When the day of the party arrived, I woke up with my stomach in knots. What if no one came? I tried to hide my anxiety as we hung a piñata from a dead tree behind our concrete patio. I set up the cake and snacks and hung pink and blue streamers with balloons across the walls. Then we sat and waited.

Precisely at the appointed time the patio door began to slide open, and kids from all over the apartment complex began to file in. You've never seen such a ragamuffin crowd for a party — and we couldn't have been more delighted. When it was time for presents, most of the kids brought things from their own toy chests — not so gently used crayons, half-colored coloring books, dirty stuffed animals. And some kids came empty-handed. We didn't care. The party was a blooming success! As I watched the broken piñata spray candy while the kids squealed in delight, tears streamed down my face.

"Thank you for this day, Lord," I sighed. "Thank you for these beautiful children, and thank you for humbling me to appreciate this imperfect moment."

I had no idea what an impression that party made on my daughter until she asked me to edit one of her college application essays. The topic was this: "Explain one of the most memorable times you've had in your life, and tell why it made an impact on you." Brooke decided to write about her birthday party. After sharing all the details of why that day was special to her, she declared, "The reason this party still impacts me is that I had the privilege of seeing how my mom humbled herself and tried to create beauty in a place that didn't often see much beauty. She loved me enough to go door to door and ask people to come."

The funny thing about a humbling posture is that even when it receives a compliment, it wants to deflect back to the One who exalts. There is a proper time to be exalted. We just need to be humble and let God choose those times.

The Reviving Posture: Posturing to Summon New Life

We have a patch of grass in our backyard that has simply refused to obey. We watered it, reseeded it, begged it — but it still defiantly refused to grow. Someone recommended a topical fertilizer that guarantees new life for dead grass. I'm all for new life, so when I grabbed the fertilizer, I let out a sweet chuckle as I read the name on the label: *Revive*. My grass is having a revival, and as I watch what was brittle turn green, I'm reminded of the hope that oozes out from being revived.

Revival is a resuscitation of sorts. It is breathing air into depleted lungs. It's taking what's dull and unresponsive and bringing it back to life. Revival is being renewed, restored, refreshed, revitalized. But what leads us to our need for revival is often a sack full of pain and negligence. Within our need for revival are postures that summon new life: reviving after failure, reviving after heartbreak, and reviving after dullness.

Reviving after failure. To experience revival after failure can be tough because it's after failure that we feel worst about ourselves. I would rather put a toothpick in my eye than fail someone, much less God. Most of us are born with a desire to please, but this desire often gets tainted as we try to gain favor from everyone — family, friends, coworkers, and even people we don't know!

The flip side of people-pleasing isn't pretty either. Those who have gotten burned from trying to please find it easy to retreat into an "I don't care what anyone thinks" attitude as they freeze out those who may try to get to know them more intimately.

The apostle Peter knew all about the need for revival. He failed Jesus in a devastating way, right when the Lord needed him most. To make matters worse, he had bragged just a few short hours before his betrayal that he would be the one the Lord could count on.

Jesus had been arrested and led away to stand before the chief priests and elders. Peter had followed at a distance, ending up in the courtyard of the high priest, where he stood warming himself at the fire.

While Peter was below in the courtyard, one of the servant girls of the high priest came by. When she saw Peter warming himself, she looked closely at him.

"You also were with that Nazarene, Jesus," she said.

But he denied it. "I don't know or understand what you're talking about," he said, and went out into the entryway.

When the servant girl saw him there, she said again to those standing around, "This fellow is one of them." Again he denied it.

After a little while, those standing near said to Peter, "Surely you are one of them, for you are a Galilean."

He began to call down curses, and he swore to them, "I don't know this man you're talking about."

Mark 14:66 – 71

We can almost feel the pain from the nerve the girl hit in Peter as he realized, in that very moment, that he had failed the One who meant everything to him. There's nothing like a behavioral meltdown to strip us of self-reliance and self-confidence. Truthfully, anything that starts with "self" needs to be stripped, but Peter's stripping was even more painful because it came from the mouths of simple folks like servant girls, maids, and bystanders. He wasn't eyeball to eyeball with the Sanhedrin; it was low-ranking people making jesting comments who backed him into his corner of denial. But what completely unnerves me is *how* he spoke at the end of this mess. He was cursing and swearing.

Peter—the man who saw Jesus in all his gleaming glory on a mountaintop, who stood next to him as he healed rotting flesh and restored blind eyes, who watched a few small fish turn into a banquet for thousands—returns to his old "pre-Jesus" behavior and curses and swears that he doesn't know him.

Have you ever thought about who wasn't at the cross when Jesus died? His mother and aunt were there; the wife of Clopas and Mary Magdalene were there; even the gospel writer John was there (John 19:25). But where was Peter?

I believe Peter was holed up in an upper room somewhere bawling his eyes out, begging Jesus to forgive him while replaying the foul cursing that had flowed so easily from his mouth. Everything about the old Peter is trying to choke out the new Peter. That's what happens when we revert to the cursing and swearing segments of our lives. The old tries to choke us and tell us there never was anything new.

Proverbs 26:11 states, "A dog returns to its vomit." I have to admit that this Scripture has always made me feel queasy. The mental image of a dog going back to lick what he's thrown up makes me sick to my stomach. Yet this is where Peter found himself. Right back in his vomit.

The good news is that Jesus doesn't leave us there. If we can posture ourselves for revival after failure, he will blow air into the empty lungs of defeat.

Although Peter wasn't at the cross the day Jesus died, he was active in the days following his death. One day, Peter announced to the other disciples, "I'm going fishing." They agreed it was a good idea and joined him out on the boat, but that night they caught nothing. As the sun came up over the beach, they heard a voice call out from the shore, instructing them to throw their nets over the right side of the boat to find what they were looking for. Not realizing at first that it was Jesus who gave the command, they put their nets overboard and hauled in an overwhelming load. John shouted to Peter, "It is the Lord!" and Peter reacted, as he always did, in dramatic fashion.

> Then the disciple whom Jesus loved said to Peter, "It is the Lord!" As soon as Simon Peter heard him say, "It is the Lord," he wrapped his outer garment around him (for he had taken it off) and jumped into the water. The other disciples followed in the boat, towing the

net full of fish, for they were not far from shore, about a hundred yards.

John 21:7 – 8

Although the boat was only a hundred yards from shore, Peter could hardly contain himself when he realized it was Jesus on the beach. He scrambled to put on his tunic and tumbled into the sea, swimming frantically to get to Jesus. It seems that Peter was always climbing out of boats to get to his Lord. The other disciples probably beat him to the shore — dry, calm, and collected — but that just wasn't Peter's style. He washed up onto the sandy beach and ran like an Olympian to get to Jesus.

As his eyes met the Lord's, Jesus kindly said, in essence, "Go and get some of the fish you just caught, and let's have some breakfast." Not a word about the denials; not a word about failing — just a compassionate invitation to share some food.

After breakfast, Jesus took Peter aside and offered restoration for the three times Peter denied him, but the power of this revival lay in the fact that Peter threw himself toward Jesus and swam for all he was worth. It's tempting to withdraw and remain paralyzed after we've let God down. We wallow in the cesspool of defeat and Satan's bullying just long enough to feel like we've drowned.

"I've asked for forgiveness too many times. God is done with giving me patience."

"I'll never get it together enough to be used by God."

"Other people are better equipped than I am."

The posture we take on after a failure isn't about the infraction; it's about the revival. If we throw ourselves toward Jesus after we've failed, he promises to revive the exasperated spirit that is prone to wander.

Reviving after heartbreak. Sometimes our failures bring about our need for reviving; other times we need revival from heartbreak we didn't ask for. Pain handed to us from another person's actions, lies, or betrayals can be some of the hardest pain to swallow. Some forms of heartbreak can blow us right out of a chair with the intensity of their throbs — the death of a loved one, the illness of a child, an unwanted divorce, a house fire, a tornado, a horrible accident.

In one of his great sermons, Oswald Chambers explains the essence of heartbreak with simple clarity:

> The first thing God does with us is to get us based on rugged reality until we do not care what becomes of us individually, as long as he gets his way for his purpose of his redemption. Why shouldn't we go through heartbreaks? Through those doorways God is opening up ways of fellowship with his Son. Most of us fall and collapse at the first grip of pain; we sit down on the threshold of God's purpose and die away of self-pity, and so-called Christian sympathy will aid us to our deathbed. But God will not. He comes with the grip of the pierced hand of his Son, and says, "Enter into fellowship with me; arise and shine." If through a broken heart God can bring his purpose to pass in the world, then thank him for breaking your heart.[14]

Reviving after dullness. The final reviving posture is one that doesn't carry the pain of failure or heartbreak but pricks and pinches like an annoying burr. Dullness in the realm of Spirit hunger can act like a knife that hasn't been sharpened. Instead of neatly slicing, it rips and shreds because of its dull blade. I can always tell when I'm in a dull place spiritually — nothing seems clear, and everything seems bland.

Most believers agree it's hardest to hear from God when our spirits feel dull. In times of great need or pain, our spirits seem to hear with crisp clarity, but when we're stuck in the mundane, it's like defrosting a freezer that has no more room for food.

In these dull times I often ask myself an important question: "Is this time truly dull, or has God allowed this period to provide me with rest or prepare me for something new?" In a culture that is addicted to action and drama, I beg God to show us the difference.

In the longest psalm recorded in the Bible, Psalm 119, the author asks God nine times to revive him. This isn't a backslidden believer, nor is it one who is unsure of what he believes. He simply wants God to breathe fresh life over him in a new way. Oh, how we long for fresh life! I love to encourage people to keep defrosting the freezers of spiritual dullness. Just the simple act of reading your Bible when you're feeling distant or praying when you don't think you're being heard starts the melting process — and before we know it, the thing that seemed like an ice chunk blocking our faith is now a small puddle on the floor.

The Expectant Posture: Posturing to Participate in a Bigger Vision

The house I grew up in had an irrigation ditch that flowed just outside our backyard fence. This was unusual for a neighborhood in the suburbs, and to the kids I grew up with, you'd have thought we had a place right on the Colorado River. We built tire swings over that ditch, inner-tubed down it in the summer, and waded in it looking for rock treasures and shimmers of gold dust.

The truth is that this ditch was pretty nasty. I remember climbing out of it one summer day, surprised to see what we thought were cute little snails on our arms. We gathered some of these "snails" into a bucket and went to our neighbor's house to ask his dad about our little bucket friends. His face turned pale as he explained that they weren't snails; they were blood-sucking leeches! To make matters worse, the ditch was home to a lot of strange animals that would thrive in the summer but then freeze into a frozen cube of flesh over the winter. One spring morning, as the ditch began to thaw, our puppy dragged in a frozen muskrat and proudly laid it at the foot of our staircase. I thought my mom would have a heart attack as she came down the stairs for her morning coffee!

Several years ago, God used the memory of that ditch to change a posture within me. There was a time in my life when I realized I was praying from a dirty ditch. I was crouched in the midst of frozen fears and overflowing doubt. There were blood-sucking leeches stuck to my faith, killing my ability to listen and to believe. The ditch I found myself in was despair, and two events in my life in particular put me there.

When my oldest daughter settled into college in California, it seemed like the perfect fit — film school, the sorority she hoped for, and roommates she enjoyed and trusted. When Bobby and I visited her in early October, we felt we had never seen her happier. But on Halloween a few short weeks later, everything changed as she was drugged at a party, led away by a college boy, and sexually assaulted. Two weeks after that fateful night, I received an e-mail detailing Brooke's recollection of what happened that night. But it wasn't until she came home for the summer that the pain hit her and our household with hurricane strength. She slipped an eight-page letter under my door one night that outlined the severity of terror she was trying to sort through. It was the type of terror that can't be described verbally.

In that letter, she explained that she was struggling with depression, alcohol, cutting, and bulimia — all a direct result of that hideous Halloween night. We went into triage mode as we sought help from several sources, attempting to unravel the black gloom of destruction that had settled over our family. Her sophomore and junior years of college were a nightmare of drunken wanderings, trying to both forget pain and remember God.

Shortly after the start of Brooke's junior year, my younger brother, Sean, was diagnosed with non-Hodgkin lymphoma. He had several tumors that presented as inoperable; one behind his eye, one near his heart, and one in the area of his groin. The clouds of winter couldn't compare to the clouds in my heart. As I watched my brother go through months of chemo and my daughter wander aimlessly in a canyon of despair, I uttered prayers that sounded more like an obituary than anything else. No expectation, no posturing to hear — just misery laced with hopeless hand-wringing.

One day as I was getting ready for work, I sensed the clear voice of God whispering to my desperate heart, "Do you believe I'm bigger than this destruction?"

I knew I wasn't believing much. As a matter of fact, I was postured to receive the continual blows of a hammer nailing down defeat.

During this time, I was reading Beth Moore's study guide, ironically titled *Believing God*, and I found a quote that challenged the trajectory of my limp faith: "God confronted me with the truth that though I had believed in him for many years, I had hardly begun to believe him."[15]

There's a big difference between believing *in* God and actually *believing* God. I knew I had to crawl out of my ditch and figure it out. So with Bible in hand each morning, I begged God to inspire me and show me what it means to adopt a posture in which I would expect him to not just be God but be *my* God — the One who is bigger than the pain that feels like it might kill me.

As I prayed with a new sense of purpose, I discovered a Scripture I had studied years earlier but had never really called to action.

> Then the LORD answered me and said,
> "Record the vision
> And inscribe it on tablets,
> That the one who reads it may run.
> For the vision is yet for the appointed time;
> It hastens toward the goal and it will not fail.
> Though it tarries, wait for it;
> For it will certainly come, it will not delay."
>
> Habakkuk 2:2 – 3 NASB

The word that held me captive in these verses was *vision*. Could it be that creating a new vision ushers in an expectant posture of prayer? Every time I had prayed about Brooke, it seemed that my mind went to worst-case scenarios in a matter of seconds. The only vision I could see was a life of misery, never really rebounding from evil but forever trying to cover the pockmarks the experience had left on her life. I ate up this Scripture. I digested it and let it nourish me.

The first thing I did was get out a tablet — an ordinary tablet, not a pretty one, because I knew my tears were going to mess it up. Scripture said to write the new vision on a tablet so the one who reads it may run with it. I was ready to run, and as I prayed about the vision I had for Brooke's life, it felt awkward to write down dreams that were the opposite of what my eyes were seeing. But God sees purpose in our writing our vision on paper. *Vision* is another word for *hope*, and if we can muster up hope when we feel like we're floating down a ditch, we're on our way to a fresh encounter with God.

As I looked at the blank, plain tablet, I allowed my mind to embrace my wildest hopes for my daughter:

- that my daughter will be free of all that plagues her and will walk in the confidence and glory of Christ
- that she will have a husband who adores her heart and shares her love for God
- that together they will minister hope and healing to those who struggle with heartaches from their past
- that she will use her talents, skills, and passion for film to flood God's love over a weary land
- that Jesus will be her comfort, strength, hope, and glory, and that God's Word will thrive in her heart and mouth.[16]

In addition to writing down the vision on paper, I searched for two or three Scriptures to describe this new eyesight I was receiving. On a quest for hope, I jotted these words next to the vision:

Now may the God of hope fill you with all joy and peace in believing, so that you will abound in hope by the power of the Holy Spirit.

Romans 15:13 NASB

Instead of hand-wringing, I was now vision praying, the prayer of an expectant posture.

I wish I could say things changed instantly. They didn't — but I did. Shortly after I began vision praying, I went out to visit Brooke. She came in late from a dance that was a disaster. She drank too much, her date ignored her, and her friends left her alone to fend for herself. When two girls dropped her off back at the apartment, I led her straight to the bathroom, where she began to get sick to her stomach. As I gently rubbed her back, I started to tumble right back down the banks of my ditch. What if things never change? What if she struggles her whole life?

Abruptly, my thought pattern shifted to the vision-filled prayers I had been praying during the past few months and to the same stark sentence God had used to get my attention in the first place: "Do you believe I'm bigger than this destruction?"

This time my limp faith was left at the doorway. "Yes!" I answered, and I began to recite the vision prayer and Scripture that I knew would be Brooke's new identity. Even if we're draped over a toilet with someone or something and not seeing the results of our vision yet, the power of this posture is the essence of hope. Hope is tonic to a sick life, a weary heart, a seasoned ditchdweller.

As the months passed, I began to see real change in Brooke. She found a church that was so alive you could feel your skin tingle when you entered it. She volunteered with the youth and helped lead a Bible study for young girls. She began to have morning time with God at Starbucks, drinking in her latte and soaking up his love. She was featured on the cover of a magazine in which she shared her story of hope and the reality of being a work in progress.

The layers of God's healing continue to wrap her like a soft blanket. God was never harsh or demanding, but patient and warm. Although several years have passed from my initial call to adopt an expectant posture, I still retreat to the faithful gift of hope in areas of life that seemed destined for ditches.

DITCH PRAYER	VISION PRAYER
• despair, defeat, failure	• hope, courage, faith
• stuck reciting only what it sees	• hopes in a God bigger than destruction
• just scrapes by, surviving the days	• excitedly looks toward the future
• fear, dread, fretting	• gutsy, tenacious, expectant

God instructed Habakkuk to write down the vision so the one who reads it may run. Before we can run with the vision, we need to create it. Although doing so may seem awkward, it's a path toward expectation rather than defeat.

1. Spill out to God everything that's on your mind regarding a person or situation. Be specific and record these thoughts. Reflect on how this situation can be touched by God and changed.

2. Ask God to reveal your part in it. What role do you play in this prayer? Sometimes you may only be required to pray; other times you may need to speak and encourage. Find Scriptures (two or three) to pray daily on behalf of your vision, and record them on something you can easily refer to. It's important to stay tenacious in your belief, regardless of what you see going on around you.

3. Mark it when you see God move in even the slightest way. Many slight ways add up to miraculous change!

Although I don't believe in formulas or in "pray this way and your dreams will come true" types of prayers, I do believe in intentionality. Praying with a purpose for a desired outcome moves us from pity to possible. As our daughter Brooke eloquently put it, "Life doesn't just wrap up with a pretty bow after we pray or give testimony. We have to keep unwrapping the gift, and let God do the rest."

A Listening Stance

Through postures of humility, revival, and expectation, we've considered ways in which we hear from God, but there's a summons that encourages an even deeper sense of listening. A summons from Jesus himself that urges, "Be still, be open, and be brave."

It's mind-blowing to think that Jesus spoke to crowds that rivaled large sporting events without the aid of a microphone. How did he grab their attention? How did he invite them to "hush" and listen?

Be Still

In back-to-back chapters in Matthew's gospel, Jesus woos the crowd in a familiar way — through their stomachs. After a full day of watching Jesus heal multitudes, the disciples tried to boss him around.

> "This is a remote place, and it's already getting late. Send the crowds away, so they can go to the villages and buy themselves some food."
>
> Matthew 14:15

It's never a good idea to be sassy with Jesus, and he bounced back with an interesting request.

> "They do not need to go away. *You* give them something to eat."
>
> Matthew 14:16, emphasis mine

In a quandary over the meager five loaves and two fish they could come up with, the disciples sheepishly gave what they had to Jesus and watched him create nourishment out of virtually nothing. But none of this would have meant a thing if Jesus hadn't been able to corral the multitudes into a posture to receive the food he had just created.

> And he directed the people to *sit down* on the grass. Taking the five loaves and the two fish and looking up to heaven, he gave thanks

and broke the loaves. Then he gave them to the disciples, and the disciples gave them to the people. They all ate and were satisfied, and the disciples picked up twelve basketfuls of pieces that were left over.

Matthew 14:19 – 20, emphasis mine

Jesus ordered the crowd to sit down. This meal wasn't going to be buffet style. He wanted to feed them, and he wanted them to know it was through him that they were filled. To truly have our Spirit hunger fed, we have to sit down — we have to *stop*; we have to *be still* — so we can receive the blessing. When we do, there will be leftovers spilling over our lives.

Prior to Jesus' order to sit, this crowd of people was probably huddled in groups, talking and milling around. Those standing closest to Jesus were watching his every move as he healed the sick and needy, but in a crowd of thousands, there are bound to be side conversations and inattention. That all changed as people now sat silently on the grass, waiting to be filled by Jesus.

It baffles me how I think I can be fed by Jesus as I blaze through my day like a parakeet set free from its cage. Flitting from place to place — conversation to conversation, stress to stress — I beg for his blessing, and then I knock him over with my flapping wings. To recline before Jesus means I must:

- stop (literally sit down and adopt a listening posture)
- focus (concentrate on verses of Scripture or concepts in the Bible that teach me)
- hear (listen for a phrase or idea that inspires new life or transformation)
- receive (like unwrapping a gift, saying thank you, and making it mine)

Jesus fed each person in that crowd. Not one man, woman, or child walked away hungry. As a matter of fact, there were leftovers to prove that when we sit and receive from Jesus, he more than satisfies.

Be Open

The second stance of listening involves being open. It does no good to be still if we're not open to what God wants to do next in and through us.

A few brief verses in Mark's gospel describe an encounter between Jesus and a man who couldn't hear and who therefore spoke with some difficulty. Something unorthodox, and frankly gross, happens as Jesus alters the course of this man's life indelibly.

> They brought to Him one who was deaf and spoke with difficulty, and they implored Him to lay His hand on him.
>
> Jesus took him aside from the crowd, by himself, and put His fingers into his ears, and after spitting, He touched his tongue with the saliva; and looking up to heaven with a deep sigh, He said to him, "Ephphatha!" that is, '*Be opened!*'"
>
> And his ears were opened, and the impediment of his tongue was removed, and he began speaking plainly.
>
> Mark 7:32 – 35 NASB, emphasis mine

It's interesting that Jesus wanted to get this man away from other people. Maybe they were in the habit of coddling him, or maybe Jesus wanted this to be strictly personal. One thing is sure: Jesus likes to have his alone time with us.

After getting this man to a place of privacy, Jesus sticks his fingers in the man's ears and then takes his own spit and places it on the man's tongue. Hanging around baseball fields, I've seen my share of spit, but this spit is different. I call it "holy spit."

Jesus takes the saliva from his mouth and places it on a tongue that doesn't form words properly. His fingers are placed in ears that don't hear. But it's the deep sigh he lets out as he speaks to heaven that stirs me. "*Be opened*," Jesus moans, and the ears and tongue touched by holy spit now work.

When my ears don't hear well, when the sounds in my ears ring out defeat and negativity, I need Jesus to put his fingers inside those ears of mine and clean them out. When my tongue is uttering words of criticism, complaint, or seductive pride, I need Jesus' saliva to rest on this tongue that is parched and twisted. It is there that we are opened and healed. May we stop to hear Jesus' deep sigh over us, and may we be open to the sway of his holy spit.

Be Brave

The final stance of listening involves being brave. Of all the most beloved Scriptures in the Bible, none is better known than the first line of Psalm 23 (NASB). "The LORD is my Shepherd, I shall not want." This line has been uttered from foxholes in bloody war battles, from ambulance stretchers, from jail cells, from school buildings under siege, from lonely beds, and from those holding checkbooks with a zero balance. I love this line of Scripture, but farther along in the psalm is a line that soars over fear. It taunts and dares fear to rear its head.

> You prepare a table before me in the presence of my enemies.
>
> Psalm 23:5 NASB

I used to think *enemies* referred to political fights between countries that don't like or understand one another, but I now realize it's more personal. We face enemies each moment we breathe. The noise we hear in our heads that tells us we can't change, that we won't grow, that we will fail. The punches Satan throws to bloody our families, relationships, dreams, and health. The lost hope triggered by addiction, procrastination, abuse, and dull neglect. These are enemies of the worst kind. Enemies that begin their torture at a low-grade temperature and slowly build to a scalding boil.

The power of Psalm 23:5 lies in the fact that God himself leads us to a dressed table. He pulls out the seat, places an embroidered napkin into our laps, and guides our chair underneath the table. He lights exquisite candles that cast a mellow glow over the table as the polished silver begs to be placed between our fingers. A plate sits before us, clean and unsoiled, like the spirit within us refreshed by the cross.

Calmly and with a sure hand, God sets this table while our enemies shriek. Smack in the heat of the hiss and snarl, right in the center of the terror, he sets a table for us. He isn't shaken. He is the essence of peace.

One of the first times I shared this concept, I asked more than 150 women to stand up and walk to the back of the room in which I was teaching. I asked for a volunteer, whom I gently led to a seat at a table while everyone circled around. The table was draped with a soft green cloth and contained etched glass candlesticks. Strings of clear beads sparkled like jewels in a crown as I silently lit the candles and placed the cloth napkin in her lap. As we looked at the beauty of the table, I reminded the ladies that this is what God beckons us to. We joined hands and bowed our heads together to soak up that moment and pray. As women began to pray, I could sense the soft rain of tears. Our prayers began as hushed praises and grew to bold pronouncements of God's goodness. One woman prayed for her wayward daughter, while another moaned over the loss of a son. Another woman shouted that she would no longer fear the coworkers who spoke poorly of her, while another broke into a verse of "Amazing Grace," which we sang together softly. All of a sudden, I realized that not only gentle tears were being shed; I could hear the sound of heaving sobs. It was as if the Holy Spirit washed over that scene with a drenching so authentic, it couldn't be mistaken for anything but glory.

In the week that followed, I received dozens of comments. "I've never felt the Lord like that!" "His presence was so real and tangible." "What a time of healing and grace!" Living proof that even though our enemies are in the midst of our lives, they are not invited to sit at the table. God has reserved that spot for *you*.

I once heard Dr. Larry Crabb say that though we are invited to sup with the King, we often crawl under the banquet table and beg for crumbs like dogs.[17] Not in this scene. We are seated at the table, and God is our waiter.

Why does this invitation to sit at God's table demand that we are brave? Isn't God the brave one to set our table in the midst of enemies? What is brave about simply sitting down?

Bravery sits with valor. Though our feet feel like running, we sit at the table, posture straight, and let God prepare. We aren't setting the table ourselves. We aren't crawling around under it. We aren't cowering in another room. We gallantly rest in the chair and let God prepare the table for us to dine.

Be still, be open, be brave — the postures from which we hear God. Henri Nouwen once wrote that the Latin word *surdus*, from which our English word *absurd* is taken, means "deaf." To be deaf to God is to live in absurdity, never knowing when he calls or what direction he leads. Nouwen also points out that our English word *obedient* comes from the Latin *audire*, which means "listening" — being "all ear." To obey God is to be all ears to his voice.[18]

Oh, that we would hear his voice, for it is in the hearing that we listen, and in the listening that we change.

chapter 10

—

HOLY PIGGYBACKS

The mood of our culture is summarized like this: "Take care of yourself and let others figure out their own lives." "Live and let live — and don't bring your problems into my backyard." But try as we may to leave each other alone, we were created to need each other. We walk alongside each other, not scamper into our foxholes and ignore each other's cries and screams for help.

Certain seasons, events, or attitudes can flatten us. In those times we need a spiritual piggyback to get back on our feet, and the piggyback we need is the lost art of intercession. I call it lost not because it can't be found but because no one seems interested in this type of prayer anymore. It's not glamorous. It doesn't draw crowds. It won't fill a stadium. But it's the heart-shaped locket that opens to a picture of priceless possession. It's the locket of maturity in which we go from "me-centered" prayer to "you-centered" petition.

Although it isn't always healthy to physically take on the burdens of those around us, spiritually we can lift, protect, encourage, and inspire others by offering them to God in a boost of intercession. Imagine the bidding to carry people's burdens on our backs through prayer instead of to fix them or to bandage them up and send them on their way. When we intercede, instead of physically jumping in to save the day, we allow the Holy Spirit to direct, correct, and clarify desires and circumstances. Perhaps the reason this type of prayer is diminishing is we become so busy trying to rearrange circumstances that as we gather the burden into our own packs, we then forget to strap that pack onto God's back. If we try to carry the pack, backs will break and hope will shatter.

Richard Foster makes this observation:

> If we truly love people, we will desire for them far more than it is within our power to give them, and this will lead us to prayer. Intercession is a way of loving others.
>
> When we move from petition to intercession we are shifting our center of gravity from our own needs to the needs and concerns of others. Intercessory Prayer is selfless prayer, even self-giving prayer.[19]

The idea of praying in a selfless manner is striking because most prayers are uttered from a self-centered stage where we are the stars. It is utter freedom to lift someone who is not me onto the stage and pull open the curtain.

The Arms of Intercession

One of the most intriguing models of intercession can be found in the life of Moses. He always had the Israelites' well-being in the forefront of his mind, but one scene is especially impressive. The Amalekites were forcefully attacking the Israelites, but Moses had a game plan that depended not only on physical might, but spiritual insight. The night before the battle he gave instruction to Joshua.

> "Choose some of our men and go out to fight the Amalekites. Tomorrow I will stand on top of the hill with the staff of God in my hands."
>
> Exodus 17:9

And here is what happened.

So Joshua fought the Amalekites as Moses had ordered, and Moses, Aaron and Hur went to the top of the hill. As long as Moses held up his hands, the Israelites were winning, but whenever he lowered his hands, the Amalekites were winning. When Moses' hands grew tired, they took a stone and put it under him and he sat on it. Aaron and Hur held his hands up — one on one side, one on the other — so that his hands remained steady till sunset.

Exodus 17:10 – 12

This is an exquisite portrayal. Joshua is fighting the battle with his hands while Moses is praying the battle with *his* hands. Each man had a role in the victory. Joshua bravely led the army, but as he glanced back, he saw three commanders standing on a hill with arms raised.

The last two times Bobby has been awarded a job coaching for a major-league team, we told the manager and his wife that we wanted to be their Aaron and Hur. We wanted to hold up their tired arms that are out there publicly fighting battles.

One of my best friends is the wife of the manager of the Houston Astros. I shared with her that each time I step on a team bus or sit on the chartered flight, I begin to intercede for her husband. Every time I see his bald head, I pray. Mondays are Bobby's arm-lifting days. He prays and fasts with the team in mind. He lifts his friend, the manager, to God with arms that help to steady him.

"Arms up" is a form of worship — and worship and intercession go hand in hand. Oswald Chambers writes, "Intercession means that we rouse ourselves up to get the mind of Christ about the one for whom we pray ... Are we so worshiping God that we rouse ourselves up to lay hold on him so that we may be brought into contact with his mind about the ones for whom we pray?"[20]

To be brought into contact with God's mind regarding the people we pray for is almost unthinkable. That's why intercession is a lighthouse on a foggy beach. If we can climb the steps inside the lighthouse, resting in the glass-encased pinnacle that overlooks the vast water, we become a prayer light that chaperones lost ships to a safe harbor.

I remember a conversation I had with a woman who sought me out after a study session. "Gari, you know I love God more than life, and you know how seriously I am committed to prayer." She grabbed my hands as tears spilled down her face. "I just don't pray well for others. I try to pray, but I feel like my mind wanders all over, and I wonder if I really care about the people I'm trying to pray for?"

I held her in my arms and shared that I honestly believed we all struggle with that. It's hard to put ourselves in the shoes of another when our own shoes fit us just fine. We spend so much time lacing up our own shoes that to put someone else's on feels a little like wearing hiking boots when you're used to running around in flip-flops.

The power of intercession is unleashed as we put ourselves in a prayer pose that invites and "takes on" the pain of someone else. To walk in someone else's shoes means we have to strap them on and feel the soles of those shoes against our own feet.

When I'm asked to pray for someone who is sick, hurting, lonely, struggling — before I pray, I must strive to put myself in the hotbed of their pain.

What does the woman who is heading for an ultrasound appointment feel after losing so many babies? How does the wife going through a third round of chemo feel as she watches the medicine cocktail drip through the IV tube? How does the young girl cope with the urge to binge and then throw up what she has ingested? What goes through the crying daddy's mind as he holds his sick child? Where do lonely people find a place to be known?

If we can identify with just a small part of what they suffer, our prayers bellow with the moans of heaven.

In the same way the Spirit also helps our weakness; for we do not know how to pray as we should, but the Spirit Himself intercedes for us with groanings too deep for words.

Romans 8:26 NASB

This is good news cradled in intimacy. The Spirit himself intercedes for us and through us with groanings that can't be confined to a spoken language. When I don't know how to pray, I ask the Spirit to groan inside me as I reflect on the life of the person who needs the prayer. Although the Spirit may not have human arms raised up to intercede, spiritual arms are raised every time I ask him to help me pray for someone in need.

Imagine the difference in our workplace if we prayed with the "arms up" approach rather than the "every man for himself" approach. What would happen if we lifted our arms for our country and our leaders rather than watching hours of mindless political jargon on TV? Picture the intimacy of teams, classes, and churches that held up each other's arms instead of casually observing as arms fell in exhaustion. The Scottish theologian P. T. Forsyth reminds us, "The deeper we go down into the valley of decision the higher we must rise ... into the mount of prayer, and we must hold up the hand of those whose chief concern is to prevail with God."[21]

FINDING THE LANGUAGE TO INTERCEDE

The night before I turned twenty-one, I was about to receive an exceptional gift. I returned home for the summer after finishing my junior year at San Diego State. (Summer has always been my favorite season in Colorado — skies the color of a robin's egg, the purple mountains' majesty stretching as far as you can see.) One of my friends was having a barbeque, sure to feature char-grilled steaks and slow-cooked beans. Since it was the night before my birthday, it seemed like the perfect way to usher in a new year.

My friends that summer were an eclectic group I had known since childhood, and a few who were grafted in with the same common love — Jesus. We were a wild bunch. Most of us had spent the previous summers at discos and bars. I was never interested in drinking, but I loved the action in a bar. I've often said that bars are a lot like churches — people gathering for a bit of fellowship. I was a competitive disco dancer who could at any moment break into dance moves at the slightest hint of an Earth, Wind & Fire tune. This particular night, I would have something to dance about.

Brand-new to the faith, I wasn't too keen on legalistic religion, but I *was* keen on Jesus, and I devoured the Bible like a starving and thirsty woman who had just crawled out of a desert. Minutes before my friends picked me up for the barbecue, I was reading from my Bible when I stumbled upon something I didn't understand. I scribbled the words from the passage on a scrap of paper and vowed to ask one of my friends to explain it later that night.

It struck me as funny how the dynamic of that friendship group had changed over the course of our years in college. Former bar-hopping disco dancers now felt there was nothing more exciting than understanding Jesus. I was the last rebel to fall, as my friends later explained they had prayed me into the kingdom with a fervor matching childbirth.

As the coals of the barbeque began to cool, I remembered the Scripture I wanted to understand, so I headed toward the back of the kitchen and pulled out the scrap of paper, trotting it out with the etiquette of a two-year-old.

To one person the Spirit gives the ability to give wise advice; someone else may be especially good at studying and teaching, and this is his gift from the same Spirit. He gives special faith to another, and to someone else the power to heal the sick. He gives power for doing miracles to some, and to others power to prophesy and preach. He gives someone else the power to know whether evil spirits are speaking through those who claim to be giving God's messages — or whether it is really the Spirit of God who is speaking. Still another person is able to speak [pray] in languages he never learned; and others, who do not know the language either, are given power to understand what he is saying [praying]. It is the same and only Holy Spirit who gives all these gifts and powers, deciding which each one of us should have.

1 Corinthians 12:8 – 11 LB, comments in brackets mine

After I belted out this Scripture with a twisted face of confusion, three of my friends grabbed my arms and whisked me off to an upstairs bedroom. They tried to explain what they thought this Scripture meant, but I felt like I was listening to radio static. Nothing was making sense. My limited understanding of prayer held me in a mixture of both confusion and intrigue. They invited me to ride home with two friends, Cindy and Randy, who would explain the Scripture in more detail, since I was definitely not interpreting their code.

We climbed into Randy's truck, all three of us perched on his bucket seat. We decided to stop at a neighborhood park near my home to unravel this mystery. As we sat on a dewy hill overlooking the swings, they began to explain that the Holy Spirit had some gifts he liked to give people who were willing to receive them. The one that intrigued me was prayer. They talked to me about a kind of prayer that was so beautiful that only God himself fully understood its cadence. "It's a prayer language," they explained, "and it's for the purpose of interceding for other people's lives."

"I want that," I whispered in a hush so tender it seemed the grass might blush. They put their arms around my shoulders and began to pray that God would see fit to bless me with this gift of prayer.

What happened next seemed almost surreal. At exactly midnight on my twenty-first birthday, I began to cry as I praised God for what I knew was transforming my limited knowledge of prayer. I cried for people I knew. I cried for people I didn't know. I cried for those in faraway places and those who lived right under my nose. There was a fresh ache for prayer, peppered with empathy and compassion. I knew then that I had a prayer language that I didn't understand. It was a language that surpassed human words and prayed straight from God's tears for mankind.

It stirs when I'm driving down the highway and see a wreck on the side of the road. Instead of being irritated by traffic, I pray for the man and woman flustered by the consequences of an accident. It springs forth when I see a lonely child on a playground, or a ballplayer walking a path of destruction. It flows when I see someone lost in a bottle of booze, or a woman beating herself up at the gym. With the fluency of a dialogue I recognize but don't always comprehend, this prayer language understands itself. It's a language of empathy, awareness, protection, and compassion. A language that surpasses mealtime grace and bedtime blessings.

I hear this language from my husband as he whispers "Let's pray" before we leave our bed in the morning. I recognize it in my close friend as she explains, "I was kneeling in prayer for you today." It resonates as my mentor says, "As I ride my exercise bike, I pray for people whose names I've written on index cards." It's a language of resolve to carry people's burdens to God rather than ignore them.

Religion has almost destroyed this sacred gift with its rules and dogma — either scaring people or lulling them into a disturbing snore. When I think back to my innocence on that grassy knoll so many years ago, I'm thankful for my ignorant bliss. It was through unstained ignorance that I received a priceless gift for which I continue to thank God. Although I don't understand everything about the gift, I understand enough to know it has offered petitions for countless people and situations for which I had no inkling how to pray. The real point of a prayer language is not the words, phrases, or dialect of the prayer but a commitment to escorting people into the arms of God with an utterance of love.

Intercession's Playlist

Like the songs on a playlist, an intercessory loop of prayer can be made for the things that tend to tie us up in knots. I see patterns in the way we intercede. We are likely to groan over our heartstrings (those we love and care for deeply), scary people and frightening things, and the salvation and growth of others.

Heartstrings

Interceding for our heartstrings can be extremely emotional because it's here that we are personally invested. These are the people we adore — the ones we carry photos of and talk about to strangers on airplanes. We have farsighted imagination that details how we hope their lives turn out. Because my imagination tends to get in the way of God's, I've come to realize that my heartstrings are best prayed for when I follow the model Jesus used for intercession.

At his last meal with the disciples before he went to the cross, Jesus allows them to hear a personal conversation he is having with his Father. It's as though we eavesdrop on the intimate groans of the Savior as he prays to the Father for *his* heartstrings — *us*.

> "But now I come to You; and these things I speak in the world so that they may have My joy made full in themselves."
>
> John 17:13 NASB

Jesus prays that his joy will be made full in those he loves. What a prayer! I'm so busy praying for circumstances to come out squeaky-clean that I forget that joy is profoundly different from happiness. Happiness needs circumstances to line up and behave in order to spill forth, while joy bubbles up within, regardless of circumstance's bossy whims.

I think back to the words of a wise woman who spoke to me shortly after I first understood the love of Jesus. She reminded me to never forget the bubbles of my salvation. I looked at her as though I was missing an important piece to the puzzle of her words. She explained that no matter what was happening in my life, the joy of loving Jesus can float up from inside me like the soapy lightness of bubbles.

I've never forgotten this image. I hold to this illustration of intercession for the ones I love. I pray for joy to well up, to surface, and to come forth from the lives of my heartstrings. Not generic joy, but the tangible joy of Jesus that isn't dependent on anything other than the essence of who he is.

> "I do not ask You to take them out of the world, but to keep them from the evil one."
>
> John 17:15 NASB

This is where intercession gets dirty. I love my heartstrings so much that I want Jesus to keep them out of the muddy parts of the world so their clothes stay perfectly clean. But that's not how Jesus prays. He wants us to stay in the world, fully loving and living — which means sometimes we will fall into the mud. But it's not mud Jesus is concerned with; he wants us to be protected from the evil one.

The evil one has one goal — to mess with humanity so completely that we stay muddied by pride, confusion, shame, and indifference. If we think we don't need God, are confused by why people make such a fuss over him, or are bound in shame and feel like we need to crawl away from him, the evil one is slinging mud chunks.

In his book *When the Enemy Strikes*, Charles Stanley writes the following:

Never forget the devil's purposes:

- To draw you away from God
- To thwart God's purpose for your life
- To deny the glory of God in your life
- To destroy you in any way he can, including physical health[22]

When we groan for our heartstrings to be protected from this mud, the result is like giving a small child a much-needed bath. Although we can't keep our heartstrings from all the places where they may get dirty, we can pray for their protection and cleansing if they get soiled.

"Sanctify them in the truth; Your word is truth."

John 17:17 NASB

When I hear a word like *sanctify*, my first reaction is to press the snooze button of my alarm clock and go back to sleep. In religious circles, the word could use a makeover. It seems we're either not sure what it means, or we're afraid it's a "whip us into shape" type of dogma. But Jesus uses the word to describe a maturity able to distinguish the truth. A process that lives and breathes with the unique rhythms of our lives — nurtured and watered by God himself. Simply put, *sanctify* means "set apart to be different." Jesus asks that we would be set apart and nurtured in truth. Then he adds the caption to the word picture he has created: *Your word is truth.*

This type of intercession understands that truth sets a captive mind free. The words of God written in the Bible heal like balm on burnt skin. It is through the pages of Scripture that truth sanctifies a weary traveler. When we shield our heartstrings with truth, a setting apart takes place. We pray they are set apart from deceit that masks as truth, from destruction that whispers excitement, and from dullness that leads to gloom.

"I do not ask on behalf of these alone, but for those also who believe in Me through their word; that they may all be one; even as You, Father, are in Me and I in You, that they also may be in Us, so that the world may believe that You sent Me."

John 17:20 – 21 NASB

Now things get juicy. The protection and the setting apart have a brawny purpose — people will be affected by the lives our heartstrings live. Their stories and words create impact. This excites Jesus so much he makes the profound wish that we will all be one, just as he and the Father are one.

This passage has been named "the high priestly prayer" because in these verses Jesus models intercession at its finest. Joy, protection, and setting apart for truth all sing a God-breathed prayer that fortifies those it covers.

Scary People and Frightening Things

The summer before I was married, I learned a stirring lesson about the power of praying for things that scare me. Each morning before work, I went for a run that took me by a beautiful house that for all practical purposes was haunted. It wasn't haunted in the sense of being abandoned and filled with spiderwebs. As a matter of fact, it was fully occupied on the inside and manicured like a city park on the outside. What haunted that house was the story that lived inside.

A girl who attended my high school had grown up in that house. She was a pom-pom girl who was a couple of years older than me. I remember studying her picture in the football program when I was trying out for the cheerleading squad. She was gorgeous — dark hair, frosted lips, and a body that screamed "10!" We all wanted to look like her. Actually, we wanted to *be* her.

Shortly after she graduated from high school, she started dating a handsome tennis pro from the local country club. They married, moved away, and had three adorable kids. I liked hearing about her, although I didn't know her well, because when all else seemed to fall apart, I could reflect on her life with a hopeful sigh and think, "See, fairy tales really do come true ..."

One day I got the news there had been a murder. The beautiful pom-pom girl was found stabbed to death in her bed. Her small son kept shaking her as he tried to wake her that morning. He was crying out, "Somebody help! Mommy has a bloody nose!" while the other two toddlers slept in their beds. Daddy was away on business and had conveniently just purchased a large life insurance policy on his wife. Police later found that the handsome tennis pro had arranged the murder of his wife, not caring that his three small children slept in the same home in which he intended a bloodbath to take place. He was found guilty and whisked off to prison, as the three little ones went to live indefinitely with their grandparents.

Each morning as I went for my run, I ran by the grandparents' house and prayed with a pain that welled from my head and stretched to my toes. From May through August, I would literally touch each fence post of that front yard as I ran by. I prayed a new mind for the three kids — a mind that wouldn't be haunted by nightmares created by their father. I prayed that the emptiness of being orphaned would be replaced with the fullness of being adopted by Christ. I prayed for strength and wisdom for the grandparents, who not only had to raise three small children but had to deal with the murder of their own daughter.

As the summer drew to a close, I was preparing to leave my hometown to meet Bobby where he was playing baseball so we could drive back to Colorado for our September wedding. I had one hour to get a run in before I had to pack for my flight, so as usual, I interceded as I ran by the house. But there was nothing usual about what happened next.

As I passed the house, I heard the giggles of small children. I turned around and saw three small kids running after me! "Hi! Hi! Hi!" they were shouting. "Can you play?"

I was stunned. Were these the little lambs I had prayed for all summer? I stopped and said, "I'd love to play. What are your names?"

We cuddled on the curb of the sidewalk a few houses from their grandparents' house as they began to tell me stories from their lives. One of the boys, the oldest, asked if he could show me pictures of their family. He ran back to the house and returned to sit smack-dab on my lap as he leafed through photos from a family Christmas a few years earlier. There was his mommy by the Christmas tree, dark hair and frosted lips, kissing her little loves. I was so unnerved I could barely speak, but I knew God was orchestrating a supernatural encounter, so I lavished love and hugs on these children who snuggled next to me with the affection reserved for those you cherish.

As time ticked by, I knew I had to go. I had a flight to catch, but

I didn't know how to end these golden moments I had been given. I scooped each child up into my arms and whispered in their ears, "Jesus adores you, and so do I." Each one of them gave me sloppy kisses and offered to give me their most prized possession — pictures of their treasured Christmas celebration. I told them those pictures were for them to keep, but I had a picture of them that I would forever lock in my mind. That thought seemed to satisfy them, and as I turned to leave — tears stinging my eyes — they ran behind me for the distance of a few houses, shouting, "We love you!" I knew that if I didn't keep running I might sprint back to them and never let go.

When I got back to my house, I dropped down onto my bed and wailed. I wailed, not because I was sad, but because I knew I had experienced a prayer gift beyond measure. All of those days I had run by that house interceding for those kids, not once had there been any sign of life. Here it was, my last day out running before we would move away from this area for good, and God saw fit to let me love on the kids I had been lifting up to him in prayer. I've never quite recovered from that. It's a gripping reminder that sometimes the things that look the scariest can be the sweetest if we just have the guts to stand in the gap and pray. The Bible states, "Do not be overcome with evil, but overcome evil with good" (Romans 12:21 NASB). The only thing that effectively overcomes evil is prayer. Revenge stirs anger, and bitterness breeds dissent — but prayer ushers in unspeakable overcoming that no evil can withstand.

I don't know what happened to these three children after I left, but I do know that for that one glorious summer, I was part of heaven's MASH unit. I was on the front lines, bandaging and cleaning out wounds with prayer, the kind of prayer that pushes away from evil's embrace.

The Salvation and Growth of Others

When you have something priceless, there's nothing like sharing it. I know many successful baseball players, the type you see on the covers of magazines, who confess that all the success in the world is empty if it can't be enjoyed with someone else. This is a glimpse of what it feels like to want others to encounter the God we sumptuously love. The problem is that most of us have no idea how to explain it, much less share it in a way that doesn't seem like we're whacking people over the head with an Amplified Bible.

Nobody likes to feel like they're being "worked on" spiritually. I know I don't. Every now and then, I come across a well-meaning believer who has made it her goal to school me. Even if her debate points are right, I find myself recoiling rather than being drawn to a new understanding of God. Shoving never gets us somewhere faster. And shoving never invites anyone to draw near to the warm embrace of God.

This is where intercession shines its brightest. Instead of shoving, intercession prays. Intercession gives God the permission to create faith where it had once been sleepy or dormant. It gives him the freedom to work on his timetable instead of inside our demanding matrix of time.

The people woven into the fabric of our lives through work, families, neighborhoods, teams, or friendships can create a sense of love that spills out into conversations and dinner parties, sporting events and side-by-side work in our yards. It's when we feel the need to shove our beliefs into their yards that we fail to experience the fullness of intercession. Interceding takes the pressure off our performance. It expresses itself as we exude a humble confidence in a God who has taken our spiritual acne and made it clear. Authenticity wins over pushiness when it comes to sharing faith, because pushiness is control wrapped in judgment. When we intercede first, God seems to open up the time and words that are right for that moment.

A few years ago, I learned an intercession lesson that continues to teach me to this day. On the streets of our city I would regularly see a woman walking with a giant backpack strapped to her back. She walked through snowstorms and rain showers and in the sizzling heat of the summer sun. I would see her on bike trails, neighborhood sidewalks, and the sides of busy streets.

The thing that drew me to her was my sense that we were kindred spirits when it came to food struggles. She was extremely thin, so thin that I worried for her health. Being a former anorexic, I felt that God was knitting my heart to hers, even though I had never met her.

I remember sitting on my bed praying with a girlfriend for all kinds of things, and suddenly I found myself praying that one day I would know this woman. Because I didn't know her name, I referred to her as "Anorexic Backpack Friend."

I prayed for a full year that we would somehow come to know each other. We had some close encounters when I wanted to stop to talk to her, but she would be on her phone as she walked or I would be driving as I passed her on the road. One summer day, I dropped off my car at the garage to have some work done. I didn't have a ride back to my house, so I happily decided to enjoy the sunshine and walk. As I rounded a corner near my home, there she was — walking exactly parallel to me. We looked at each other and smiled a polite hello, but she passed me with what seemed like the speed of a cheetah. As I tried to follow a step or two behind, I found myself in a prayer war.

"Talk to her. This is your chance!" one part of me shouted, while another voice screamed, "Yeah, right, what are you going to say? Just be quiet, and let her go on ahead!"

I wasn't about to waste a year of begging God to let me know her, so I did the sanest thing I could think of. I walked behind her as if I were stalking her. After rounding two streets at a panting pace, I finally called out, "I'm really not trying to follow you; I actually live at the top of this street!" She smiled with a sweet smile and walked next to me, introducing herself as Sarah. We asked a few polite questions, which seemed to lead to an instant connection — the kind that a year's worth of interceding served up on a platter. By the time we got to the top of the street, she shared with me about some of her food struggles, and I shared with her my history. We also talked about families and interests, when suddenly she looked at me and said, "Would you like to go mountain climbing with me this weekend?" I stuttered back a loud, "Sure!" as we exchanged numbers and arranged the details of our climb.

As I opened the front door to my house, I fell on the floor in worship. Had that really just happened? I had prayed the span of a year for this unknown person I wanted to befriend. We walked the distance of a block together and ended up with a date to climb a mountain together!

Our climbing date was a glorious mixture of deep conversation and breathtaking views. We shared our lives with each other and promised to meet again soon. We began meeting weekly for coffee, which resulted in a trusted friendship that had little to do with food and more to do with God's potent love.

I invited Sarah to a Bible study that met in my living room the following summer. I also grafted her into a group of ragtag prayer women who met in my bedroom every other week to pray. The transformation in Sarah was nothing short of stunning. She became a lover of God's Word and a leader of women. I'm certain that if I had forced myself in front of her with an agenda that was different from God's, I would have pushed her away.

Intercession begs that God's agenda for salvation and growth will be the focus, not our need to gather people around our personal profiles.

So it is with respect and prayer that we shoulder one another's loads in a holy piggyback that enables the person on our backs to get a clear view of the road ahead. We lift them up and love them, knowing that God crafts the road map and designs the journey.

The Cost of Prayer

Intercession isn't for sissies. It takes spiritual grit to stay locked in on the needs of others. So many things can happen to divert our groans, yanking our arms out of the air.

For some, intercession disappears when the person prayed for shows no improvement or when a situation seems to take a turn for the worse. It's here that intercession alone isn't enough. Consider what the apostle Paul wrote.

> Be anxious for nothing, but in everything by prayer and *supplication* with thanksgiving let your requests be made known to God.
>
> Philippians 4:6 NASB, emphasis mine

Paul adds a word to the task of prayer that revs it up like a race car's engine at the starting line. To add *supplication* to intercessory prayer "means to ask with earnestness, with intensity, with perseverance. It is a declaration that we are deadly serious about this prayer business. We are going to keep at it and not give up."[23]

When we take on the burdens of others through prayer, because of our lightweight objection to feeling uncomfortable, it is with supplication that we push forward with no mind to our own flesh. The supernatural thing about intercession is that it has no boundaries. In real life we have to live within boundaries, or we will get swallowed up in the gulf of human nature, which has a penchant for abuse, taking advantage, and neglect. Intercessory prayer has none of these obstacles, for it operates in a different realm.

While our natural human tendency is to try to fix, to ease, and to control, prayer is the meadow in which we can romp, cry, hope, and dream without the blemish of behavioral quirks. We are free to pray for things for others they aren't capable of praying for on behalf of themselves.

chapter 11

FROM QUESTIONS TO RESOLVE

*I*t's embarrassing to think of the soapboxes I used to stand on before I had kids. I remember boldly proclaiming that my children would never eat sugar, and I certainly would never use the TV as a babysitter. When my two daughters were born thirteen months apart, it didn't take long for me to be shrieking at the top of my lungs, "Take your bowl of Fruit Loops and sit in front of that TV screen!" So much for soapboxes.

It was this way with patience as well. Often I had heard mothers gruffly resorting to the old tried-and-true phrases to get their kids to stop asking questions. As for me, "I'll answer any questions my sweet angels pose," I smugly thought. That was all well and good until one day my soapbox bubbled into lather the size of Texas. I was driving down the road, trying to piece together a coherent thought while my little lambs were bombarding me with whys and what fors.

"Why do roads curve, Mommy?" "What are leaves made of?" "Why does the stoplight change from red to green?" "Where do all the bags of trash go?" "Why is the sky blue and dirt brown?"

Unable to restrain myself in this blizzard of confusion, I blurted out, "Because God wants it that way!" Shockingly, that seemed to quiet their barrage — at least for the rest of the day.

I can only imagine the questions God gets slammed with every millisecond. Like the back and forth motion of windshield wipers on a rainy day, some questions wipe clear a spattered window, while others seem to slosh the rain into an even sloppier mess.

The good news is that God doesn't get frustrated with our questions. He's not giving us a bowl of sugary cereal and sitting us in front of a TV to get us to shush up. As a matter of fact, most of the time God's reaction to our wonderment has a "bring it on" tang to it. Other times, we hear a simple, "Because I know a better way."

One of the finest word pictures in the Bible used to portray this liaison between Creator and created is that of clay. As a potter shapes and massages a formless blob into a useful piece of beauty, so God molds and crafts us into his works of art.

> This is the word that came to Jeremiah from the LORD: "Go down to the potter's house, and there I will give you my message." So I went down to the potter's house, and I saw him working at the wheel. But the pot he was shaping from the clay was marred in his hands; so the potter formed it into another pot, shaping it as seemed best to him.
>
> Then the word of the LORD came to me. He said, "Can I not do with you, Israel, as this potter does?" declares the LORD. "Like clay in the hand of the potter, so are you in my hand, Israel."
>
> Jeremiah 18:1 – 6

Years ago, I had the pleasure of watching a master potter work with his clay. He grabbed a shapeless handful of gray clay and began dousing it with water. It was slippery, and little chunks of it sloughed off and fell to the ground. He then slapped the gray mass onto his wheel. It began spinning in circles so fast that water spritzed the walls, the floors, and the potter himself. As it began to take shape, I was thinking, "Wow, it really looks good. I think he's almost done." Without warning, the potter stopped the spinning, grabbed the good-looking mass that now resembled a pot, slapped it back into a formless sphere, and started over! All who were watching let out an audible gasp as we realized this potter meant business. He wasn't satisfied with a pot that looked good; he wanted it to be brilliant from the inside out, strong for useful service and stunning to behold.

God shapes us this same way. Just when we think we look good, he reshapes areas of our lives that need to be pliable. He soaks us with living water so we can be changed.

In the Hands of the Potter

The essence of why this process is so difficult rests on a few *pottery principles* that seem to be the catalyst for most of the questions we have.

Pottery Principle #1

The first pottery principle is this: *We don't want to be the clay; we want to be the potter.* Human nature is always asking one fundamental question: Who's in charge? Once we figure this out, we invariably try to manipulate this relationship for our own benefit.

When we lost our job with the New York Yankees a few years ago, the person who voiced the comments that led to our firing didn't speak to the manager or to his boss, the general manager. He spoke directly to the ownership group that was at the top of the power pyramid. If you really want to make something happen, you go to where opinions matter.

After teaching elementary school for fifteen years, I worked as a staff developer and national consultant. I could walk into a classroom anywhere in the country, and after five minutes, I could tell exactly who was in charge. Teachers who aren't in charge have typically given over the reins of their classroom to those who exhibit the worst behavior.

Even sweet kindergartners are on a quest to see who's in charge, and they will seek to take over if no one else leads.

Bobby and I saw this dynamic play out within our own family setting. While standing atop another one of my soapboxes, I proclaimed, "I will only discipline with kind words. No spankings or useless time-outs!" Lather, lather . . .

When our oldest daughter, Brooke, was two, we lived in a hundred-year-old home on a plot of ground that had once been a chicken farm. It was a fabulous home, but it had a steep wooden staircase that was tricky to descend. Brooke had gotten into the dangerous habit of climbing out of her bed and pitter-pattering throughout the house, putting herself in danger of tumbling down those stairs. One time we found her roaming around at 2:00 a.m.! No amount of kind instructions or pleading stopped this behavior, and we found ourselves once again dismantling another soapbox. We decided we were going to use a wooden spoon as a spanking threat, hoping we never would need to use it.

Each night, Bobby would curl up with our lamb in her bed and go over the game plan. "Sweetie, what happens if you get out of your bed at night?" "Spankin' with the wooden spoon, Daddy," she would gush with a smile as wide as a watermelon slice. "That's right, precious," Bobby would respond. "Daddy doesn't want to use the wooden spoon, so don't get out of your bed tonight, right, sweetie?" "Right, Daddy!" she would tweet as she nuzzled up to his cheek with a wet kiss.

Every night for a solid month — pitter-patter, pitter-patter — without fail. Bobby would look at me with a face etched in disbelief as that wooden spoon got more action than it would have in a bakery!

It took four weeks for her to figure out who was in charge, and after she made that leap of understanding, the spoon went back to taking up residence in a drawer.

Adults are no different. We will push and prod until we figure out who's in charge. Ironically, the answer to that question of who is in charge never changes: God is. We can be pliable clay in his weathered hands, or we can be clay that needs to be reshaped and drenched because it refuses to be formed like the potter wants it to be.

No one understood this pottery principle better than Jonah. In four brief chapters in the Bible we see a man who went to insane lengths to run from the one in charge. God allowed Jonah's running to take him to some dark places (the stomach of a fish is about as dark as it gets) before he finally relinquished the one thing that held him captive — his stubborn will.

> The word of the LORD came to Jonah son of Amittai: "Go to the great city of Nineveh and preach against it, because its wickedness has come up before me."
>
> But Jonah ran away from the LORD and headed for Tarshish. He went down to Joppa, where he found a ship bound for that port. After paying the fare, he went aboard and sailed for Tarshish to flee from the LORD.
>
> Jonah 1:1 – 3

No monkey business here — Jonah is running for all he's worth. In today's language, this conversation may have sounded like this:

God: "Jonah, I want you to go to Las Vegas and pour my love and grace on a city that needs help."
Jonah: "Not on your life! I'm booking a ticket for Idaho."

This response makes me blush with understanding as I chew on the question, "Why do we run from God?"

Fear. One of the reasons we run is simply that *we're afraid.* When God leads us to mountains that hold out to us challenge and adventure, fear torments us with currents that pull us away.

"Let God use someone else. I'm not up to this."

"I'm not gifted in this way. I don't know what to do."

"If I move in this direction, what will the outcome be for my family and my future?"

Fear spews with the force of a geyser, restructuring God's confidence in us, leaving us spouting phrases that reject God's invitation to splendor.

Insecurity. Another reason we run is that *we feel unequipped*. I can't tell you the times I have rolled around in this mud. For years, I prayed I would be a published author, and after decades of writing for small newspapers and a sports magazine and contributing to a few small book projects with other authors, it was finally time to cross over into this territory myself. The problem was that I didn't feel smart enough. Every conference I attended added salt to that wound as we rehashed the message, "It is so hard to get published!" Truthfully, the task of writing a book seemed like climbing the Himalayas.

I remember talking to Bobby's best friend about my desire to write. He's a famous movie writer, producer, director, and comedian. After telling him for years about my passion and sharing every excuse in the book as to why I couldn't write, he looked at me one day and said, "Gari, bake the cake! You keep talking about all the ingredients. Just go bake the cake!"

I was fuming as I sputtered more reasons why I couldn't "bake" (full-time job, raising three kids, health issues, financial concerns, blah, blah, blah). Finally I said to the Lord, "OK, let's bake."

The problem with feeling unequipped is that it's not God who puts this idea into our heads. The author of Hebrews delivers this beautiful benediction.

> Now the God of peace, who brought up from the dead the great Shepherd of the sheep through the blood of the eternal covenant, even Jesus our Lord, *equip you in every good thing to do His will*, working in us that which is pleasing in His sight, through Jesus Christ, to whom be the glory forever and ever. Amen.
>
> Hebrews 13:20 – 21 NASB, emphasis mine

God equips us for every good thing we will ever do. Instead of lacing up our sneakers to run because we don't think we're smart enough, good enough, pretty enough, confident enough, peaceful enough, or pulled together enough, what if we simply stated, "God has equipped me for every good thing, and *that's* enough"?

Pride and self-centeredness. Not only do we feel afraid and unequipped; *we want to be our own boss*. We don't like being asked to do things that don't fit into our Day-Timer or smartphone calendar. Kids are famous for shouting to one another, "You're not the boss of me!" How often do we shout that same line to God in defiance of his love and authority? He *is* the boss of me. He is the boss of everyone. And even when we run for the hills (or the sea, in Jonah's case), God persuades us to let his will win over our need to fight it.

One of the things I admire about Jonah is that even though his pride and selfishness led to his flight, he owned up to the fact that he was running. Once Jonah boarded the ship to Tarshish, the Lord unleashed a great wind on the sea, causing a storm so severe that the ship was about to break into pieces. The sailors were beside themselves, throwing cargo overboard to try to save each other. And where was Jonah? Sound asleep in the hold of the ship. When the captain roused him, he began asking him a string of desperate questions.

> "What kind of work do you do? Where do you come from? What is your country? From what people are you?"
>
> Jonah 1:8

Jonah answered with the swagger of a rebellious Sunday school student.

> He answered, "I am a Hebrew and I worship the Lord, the God of heaven, who made the sea and the dry land."
> This terrified them and they asked, "What have you done?" (They knew he was running away from the Lord, because he had already told them so.)
>
> Jonah 1:9 – 10

You have to hand it to Jonah; at least he didn't make excuses to the sailors. They knew exactly what he was running from. In a gallant effort to save the crew, Jonah told them to throw him overboard, but the sailors kept searching for other options. When there seemed to be no other way to calm the storm, they picked him up and threw him into the sea. Instantly the sea stopped raging, but the Lord appointed a great fish to swallow Jonah, and he was trapped inside the belly of that beast for three days and nights. It's crazy to think he would rather be thrown into a raging sea than apologize to the Lord for running and rebook a ticket to Nineveh.

I've often wondered what Jonah's experience in the belly of a fish must have felt like. Scientists believe the fish was noncarnivorous. In other words, it wasn't a meat eater. It didn't have the digestive enzymes that a meat-eating fish did; if it had, Jonah would have been killed instantly. Some of the largest mammals on earth are whales, and they simply open their huge mouths wide as plants, plankton, and wildlife rush into the stomach cavity.

After I spoke on this topic one day, a man approached me and shared a story he had been told of a sailor who had fallen overboard at sea. The sailor was swallowed by a whale that was harpooned and cut open two days later. The man was found alive inside the belly — shaken by the experience but alive to tell about it.

Some people think Jonah's experience was just a Bible tale, much like the story of Cinderella or Snow White, but Jesus himself refers to this encounter with anything but fairy-tale language.

> "As Jonah was three days and three nights in the belly of a huge fish, so the Son of Man will be three days and three nights in the heart of the earth."
>
> Matthew 12:40

If Jesus quotes this as truth, that's enough for me. And really, it's what happened to Jonah inside the lining of a stomach that resonates for all of us who are prone to run. Jonah has a potter and clay moment as he finally allows his stubborn will to be reshaped by God's capable hands. From inside that dark belly he utters these words:

> "While I was fainting away,
> I remembered the LORD,
> And my prayer came to You,
> Into Your holy temple ...
> But I will sacrifice to You
> With the voice of thanksgiving.
> That which I have vowed I will pay.
> Salvation is from the LORD."
>
> Then the LORD commanded the fish, and it vomited Jonah up onto the dry land.
>
> Jonah 2:7, 9 – 10 NASB

Oh, the fish we end up in as we run from God! He may not be calling us to go and preach in Las Vegas, but he may be nudging us to give up a precious habit that is secret or destructive. He may be asking us to trust him for something bigger when we are clinging to a smaller version of his will. He may be hoping we'll say yes to a challenge that will bring untold blessings to our family and to the generations that follow. Many storms — and many hours spent in dark bellies — can be avoided if we say yes to the potter and surrender to his exquisite, clay-stained hands.

Pottery Principle #2

The second pottery principle is this: *We struggle with the shape the potter chooses for us; we want to look like the **other** pots.*

One of the reasons I think it's especially difficult to be a woman today is that we are whacked upside the head with images of what we *should* be. We should look a certain way — tall, thin, and alluring. We should function a certain way — balancing schedules, work, kids, husbands.

We should love God a certain way — look good at church but never admit we feel unconnected or alone.

My grandmother had a twin sister, and the two of them together made a bull in a china shop look graceful. One of the things I loved most was sitting in my grandma's kitchen, listening to the wisdom they shared on life topics. My great-aunt would always start a sentence with, "You know what *they* say ..." — and a comment would emerge that you just knew you had to adopt into your world outlook. One day my mom and I stopped her in midsentence and asked, "Who exactly are *they*?" It dawned on us that so much of what we cling to as truth comes from a mystical "they" who don't know a thing about us or about the pot God has purposed our life to resemble.

Some principles God braises in our lives, and some he marinates. This has been a marinating principle I have soaked in — hoping the heat of the grill will bring out a sweet flavor.

Bobby was a first-round draft pick, which meant that a lot of baseball teams wanted him and were going to pay top money to get him. At the time, we were poor college students who didn't have much grasp of what was happening. I remember driving up in Bobby's silver Pinto station wagon to the Beverly Hills Country Club, where we were going to meet with a prospective agent. (I'm sure the valet driver who then took the car howled as he parked it next to cars that cost more than our college education.) I wore the one dress I owned and climbed out of the car doing deep breathing exercises to keep my nervous lungs working. A few short weeks later, Bobby was drafted and flew off to play minor-league ball on the East Coast. After a quick two years in the minor leagues, Bobby was tapped to play in the big leagues for the New York Yankees. We were newlyweds as I finished school and joined him in the Big Apple, which really felt more like the Mushy Banana to me, as I didn't know a thing about city living, much less living near the Bronx. We rented an apartment in Hackensack, New Jersey, which was furnished with all the leopard print and animal wall paintings you could hope for.

Each day, I went to the ballpark and worked on making new friends and figuring out how to be a good wife in this zoo-like environment. Some of the women were wonderful, and some were the epitome of ice princesses — cold, very icy, and mean.

One of the wives caught my eye immediately as I watched her walk to her seat each night. She was beautiful — skinny with great skin and hair — and her husband was wildly successful. He never seemed to struggle to get hits, which was a nightly battle for Bobby as we prayed to keep our job with the big league club. She wasn't very well liked on the team after a series of events that demonstrated her icy heart, but I looked at her and lusted for just about everything she had and did. I said to the Lord quite plainly, "I want *her* pot, not this plain pot you made me to be!"

A few months into that season, we found out we were both pregnant. I was elated, and together we shared our excitement as we talked about due dates, doctors, and baby clothes. But shortly into my pregnancy I began to bleed and painfully lost our first child to a miscarriage.

Each night at the ballpark, I listened to my friend moan and complain about being pregnant. At this point, I was functioning in a low-grade depression; Bobby traveled constantly, and I was alone in a city that never sleeps. I tried to comfort her but often thought, "Doesn't she know how much I would give to be in her place?" In the midst of that pain, I was now shouting to God, "I want *her* pot!"

Over the course of the next few years I did get pregnant again, and we shared the joy of watching our children run to their daddies after a ballgame. Although she was still icy, I gave her the first Bible she ever owned and threw a baby shower for her when no one else wanted to. Shortly after our fifth season with the Yankees, we were traded and lost contact. Her husband was outrageously successful in the game, while we limped along, trying to piece together minor-league deals and then settling into coaching. And I was continuing to say, "Their pot sure looks good, God. I wish ours was as shiny."

Almost twenty years had passed when one day I glanced at the headlines and saw something so shocking that it almost knocked my laptop out of my hands: a photograph of this woman who seemed to have it all. The once-beautiful face was now wrinkled and worn. She looked like a wounded animal — scraggly hair and eyes that lamented a life she had lost yet longed to regain.

Her marriage to the star player had broken up. I don't know why her life fell apart, but I fell to my knees to ask God to comfort her and to thank God for the precious, humble way he chose to craft my pot. "Thank you for *this* pot, dear God," I uttered. "This is the only pot I want to be."

I love those occasions when we have clarity to see God's providence in pottery making, but it's easy to get caught looking at other people's pots. After Peter denied knowing the Lord, he seemed to go missing in action while trying to come to terms with his fickle heart. Jesus restored his purpose in a series of shepherding cues that he laid over Peter's life in a conversation they had on the beach.

> When they had finished eating, Jesus said to Simon Peter, "Simon son of John, do you love me more than these?"
>
> "Yes, Lord," he said. "You know that I love you."
>
> Jesus said, "Feed my lambs."
>
> Again Jesus said, "Simon son of John, do you love me?"
>
> He answered, "Yes, Lord, you know that I love you."
>
> Jesus said, "Take care of my sheep."
>
> The third time he said to him, "Simon son of John, do you love me?"
>
> Peter was hurt because Jesus asked him the third time, "Do you love me?" He said, "Lord, you know all things; you know that I love you."
>
> Jesus said, "Feed my sheep."
>
> John 21:15 – 17

Peter's purpose was restored as Jesus laid a fresh layer of healing over each time he had denied him. But what happened *after* this restoration amuses me.

Jesus shares a sentence with Peter that could flatten him like a sheet of thin notebook paper, but Peter is so busy looking at someone else's pot that it sails right by him.

> "Very truly I tell you, when you were younger you dressed yourself and went where you wanted; but when you are old you will stretch out your hands, and someone else will dress you and lead you where you do not want to go." Jesus said this to indicate the kind of death by which Peter would glorify God. Then he said to him, "Follow me!"
>
> John 21:18 – 19

This is heavy stuff, as Jesus explains to Peter that his life is now not his own. Jesus knows how Peter is going to die. Ironically he would be crucified like Jesus but ask to be executed upside down because he didn't consider himself worthy to die the same way Jesus did.

Never mind that as Jesus explains this perilous event, Peter's head is cocked back to look at someone else's pot.

> Peter turned and saw that the disciple whom Jesus loved was following them. (This was the one who had leaned back against Jesus at the supper and had said, "Lord, who is going to betray you?") When Peter saw him, he asked, "Lord, what about him?"
>
> Jesus answered, "If I want him to remain alive until I return, what is that to you? You must follow me."
>
> John 21:20 – 22

Here Peter is, face-to-face with the God he loves, and he's nosing around in God's plan for someone else. Oh, how I love this man! He always brings me back to the authenticity of the Bible, and how thankful I am for imperfect vessels that God humorously still sees fit to use! Even if we're inclined to look at other people's pots, it's comforting to know that we lean up next to the potter, who lovingly redirects our gaze to him.

Pottery Principle #3

The third pottery principle is this: *We don't like to submit to the pain of shaping and reshaping; we want the process of becoming useful to be painless, quick, and explainable.*

I don't know anyone who loves pain. I've never heard a single person say, "I can't wait to feel miserable!" But sometimes pain is the best road map toward growth, and without growth, we are immature slugs that slosh through life. Consider these helpful thoughts from author James MacDonald:

> God's goal is always that the pain he brings would take us to a better place. Surgeons don't lament the pain of their procedure. Just as a physician must wound to heal … just as the skin must be cut to remove a tumor … so God inflicts pain to ensure that our hearts will make their way finally to the only fountain of true joy — God himself.[24]

Reading these words got me thinking: A mechanic doesn't have to justify taking apart the engine of a car to find a malfunction. A gardener doesn't think twice about chopping off branches to stimulate growth. A parent would never hesitate to reach out and roughly grab a child to save them from oncoming traffic. Yet with God, we act as though he owes us an apology for allowing our lives to experience pain or discomfort.

There is a word we don't typically apply to Jesus, and that word is *sorrow*. Isaiah described Jesus as "a man of sorrows and acquainted with grief" (Isaiah 53:3 NASB), yet we don't see this verse plastered on bumper stickers.

Although we dance around sorrow, it is through this tryst that we emerge useful. Oswald Chambers shares these thoughts:

> Sorrow burns up a great amount of shallowness, but it does not always make a man [or woman] better. Suffering either gives me my self or it destroys my self ... You always know the man [or woman] who has been through the fires of sorrow and received himself, you are certain you can go to him in trouble and find that he has ample leisure for you ... If you receive yourself in the fires of sorrow, God will make you nourishment for other people.[25]

Receiving ourselves in sorrow leads to freshness in our lives. The freedom to have an expectant outlook rather than a bitter one. One thing I know about sorrow is that it either pushes us toward hope or abandons us in anger.

One day I had gone to see the counselor my daughter was seeing and explained that I felt like I couldn't catch my breath. Every time I tried to fill my lungs with air, a wave of panic seemed to suck the oxygen right out as I thought about my daughter's heartache and my fear of losing my little brother to cancer. She quietly looked at me and said, "You can't catch your breath because pain has overtaken breathing. You now understand the fellowship of sorrow."

It's funny how I had always been the cheerleader type. "Pray Scripture! Think positive! God is good!" To be sure, all of these are positive statements, but when we're in the *fellowship of sorrow*, cheerleading only unnerves our already shattered bravado.

Each day I scoured the Scriptures for glimpses of sorrow. I especially needed to see how Jesus handled this fellowship that I knew he was intimately acquainted with.

Jesus prayed. He wept. He cried out to heaven. He loved. He healed. He fed. He served. He cleansed. And finally, he died. His dealings with sorrow led him squarely back to a place of mysterious joy.

The joy certainly wasn't in the blister of circumstance. The thought of finding joy in cancer, abuse, rape, alcoholism, addiction, bingeing, or betrayal is absurd. The joy comes from the *fellowship of sorrow*. Those who travel in this fellowship know the strange delight when pain no longer outweighs promise.

The promise of a hope. The promise of a future. The promise of plans that whisper eternity. Those promises, settled in hope, have the capacity to look past sorrow to the joy set before them. For it is in that joy that we are nourished and can provide nourishment for others from the kindling fodder of our pain.

The Whys and What Fors

A young woman from Australia contacted me after reading my book *Truly Fed*. She shared that after years of struggling with overeating and purging, after years of hating the way she interacted with food, she had finally come to the point where she wanted to change more than she wanted to binge. She called her touch point of clarity a *compass moment* — where all the questions she had moaned for years lost their obsessive appeal.

The whys and what fors of life may begin naturally, but if we stay stuck in the grip of questions that have no answers, we miss the compass moments that can lead to new routes and landscapes. Typically, most questions have three stages: Why? What for? What now?

Why questions are laced with the shout, "Why me?" "Why us?" In pottery terms it goes like this: "Why is my pot cracked? "Why isn't my pot smoothly painted?"

Bobby and I recognized a marker of maturity when we could look upon the why question and shout back, "Why *not* me? Why do I think I should be exempt from circumstances that squeeze hardened grapes into sweet wine?"

Although *why* questions start the initial quest for relief, the *what for* type seems to lasso our reasoning. *What for* really entails asking what good can possibly come from a befuddling circumstance.

As a child, I asked God this question for fifteen years. I saw no good result from my dad's car accident. It was tragic, that's all. One piece of tragedy layered over another as I saw multiple lives sink like wounded ships in the aftermath of that one ill-fated night. I brooded over that question. I stewed over that question. I shouted it when no one was listening and whimpered it into my pillow at night.

Much to my surprise, when I asked Jesus to take over the reins of my life in college, this question was the first one he answered. He didn't go after the eating disorder that had placed me deep in the dungeon; he didn't go after the insecurity holding its one hand over my eyes and belting me in the gut with its other. He went after a question I had wailed most of my childhood. One I had given up hope of ever understanding.

In answering my *what for*, he posed a few *what ifs*. "What if I could forgive my dad for that night that changed the course of our family's life? What if I could trust God to restore a relationship with a father I never really knew? What if I trusted God to heal the relationships that broke and splintered as a result of the accident that took more than my father's legs?"

The interesting thing about *what for* is that when it changes to *what if*, the next question becomes *what now*. *What now* is empowering as it shifts from past puddles to dry ground.

Zechariah asked this question of the angel Gabriel when he announced that he and Elizabeth would soon have a son. This pain had been the source of *whys* and *what fors* that spanned decades as he and his wife struggled with infertility. "What now?" echoed from the temple as Zechariah moved forward in fresh resolve (Luke 1:18).

Moses asked a *what now* question after God instructed him to lead a chosen people toward freedom. Moses moved past the *whys* and *what fors* to ask, "What now?" as he spoke with God about his stuttering problem (Exodus 4:14).

Joseph asked a *what now* question as he chose to believe God rather than settle into strangling self-pity after hearing that Mary was pregnant with a child who wasn't his but rather was humanity's.

Pain gives birth to purpose. It is here that we realize questions aren't the point; God's movement is. Questions can lead to trust, as long as we don't get stuck in their windy vortex.

A MATTER OF CLAY

The miracles Jesus gave as gifts followed no formula. There wasn't a prescriptive feel to them, as each one had a unique sense of story that fit the person it was intended to impact. It is fitting that the miracle John described revolved around clay.

> As he went along, he saw a man blind from birth. His disciples asked him, "Rabbi, who sinned, this man or his parents, that he was born blind?"
>
> "Neither this man nor his parents sinned," said Jesus, "but this happened so that the works of God might be displayed in him" ...
>
> After saying this, he spit on the ground, made some mud with the saliva, and put it on the man's eyes. "Go," he told him, "wash in the Pool of Siloam" ... So the man went and washed, and came home seeing.
>
> John 9:1 – 3, 6 – 7

A boy born blind brings torrents of tears and disappointment. To eyes that can't see the parents who adore him. And to eyes that can't see the arms that hold him.

When the disciples stumbled onto this troubling scene, they wanted to make sense of it — so placing the blame on sin seemed the logical sport. But Jesus says something so counter to the cultural verdict that droplets of hope are sneezed all over the stuffy outlook.

"This condition has absolutely nothing to do with this man's behavior or with the behavior of his parents," declares Jesus in essence. "It has come about so that the works of God can be showcased in him." If ever we needed something to put perspective on our *whys* and *what fors*, this statement deals a crushing blow to the depression of empty wondering.

All of us are blind in one way or another. All of us, at the end of our lives, will look back over certain seasons and wonder why this or why that. But Jesus makes clay from his saliva, puts it over our empty eyes, and says, "Go and wash — for the clay that I use will display God's glory."

It's a bit funny that our eyes need to be covered with *his* clay. We can't create the clay ourselves; that would be Play-Doh. His clay draws out infection. It restores sight where the focus had been blind. It brings dynamic new life and brilliant color to eyes that are used to seeing the same shade of gray.

If we're honest with ourselves, our lives are his clay. I'd rather be on the wheel in his hands than in a display window, feebly boasting about my own clumsy craftsmanship.

chapter 12

—

GETTING IN
THE PARADE

Moving from bystander to disciple is a bit like attending a parade. There are those who stand on the side of the road, oohing and aahing as the floats roll by; and then there are those who are in the parade, waving, marching, and making music. Those who are in the parade are not merely watching the action; they're helping to create it. To be a disciple is to be a part of God's action, to be a vibrant tool in the course of events he is orchestrating. A bystander watches, and a disciple participates.

I remember when I joined the parade instead of just sitting on the sidelines watching it. I had seen God move two mountains in my life — healing my obsession with food and showing me how to forgive my dad. Although I was a new Christian, nobody was going to snuff out this freedom and hope that now rang out from the rooftop of my life.

I decided to let people know I was hosting an informal Bible study in my dormitory. Much to my surprise, people came! We crammed into my tiny room, sitting on the floor and bed; some even stood because they couldn't find any other place to perch. The first thing out of my mouth after we prayed were these memorable words: "Please turn to the book of Filipinos." I'm no scholar, but the last time I looked there was no book of Filipinos in the Bible. Filipinos are people from the Philippine Islands in the Pacific. I was as red as a pomegranate as one of the girls in the room, a seasoned Christian, gently giggled. "Do you mean Philippians?" she whispered. I tried to act like I meant to say Filipinos to be funny, but truthfully, I didn't have a clue what I was doing. All I knew was I had to get in the parade. I was no longer satisfied to watch from the curb of belief; I needed to be in the action.

I carried my Bible with me for years, rarely leaving home without it. It was in my backpack, suitcase, purse, diaper bag, and briefcase. It was on my desk at school when I taught, and on my nightstand when I slept. I became a student of its teachings and a lover of its touch. It was through these worn pages that I realized this is how Jesus attracts us. He stirs in that place in our lives where our need and passion are greatest; and in that spot, he christens us ready to join his parade.

Disciples can be overlooked because the best of them don't want a spotlight on *their* procession; they want one person on the float to get the glory — and that person is Jesus Christ.

Of all the disciples I've known, one stands out like a weather vane atop a sturdy barn. His name was Donnie, the janitor at Peabody Elementary School. Donnie was a man of small stature. His dark hair and eyes etched his olive skin and strong jaw. Although he was small, he could carry twice his weight, and I think he singlehandedly ran that school.

Donnie could be seen corralling naughty boys and putting them to work picking up trash or reconstructing the playground. He could plant a tree or hold the hand of a lost kindergartner, but I'll never forget the day Donnie instructed me like Jesus himself would have.

Bobby was facing yet another year of uncertainty with his work in baseball; his year-to-year contract had expired, leaving us without work — again. I took my lunch outside to sit against a brick wall by the dumpster, in no mood to make small talk in the teacher's lounge. Donnie came out carrying a load of trash, and he saw me leaning against the wall crying. He asked what was bothering me, and I sniffled an embarrassed response. Donnie looked at me, trash bag in one hand, grace in the other, and offered a response that begged for a pulpit. "Gari," he said, "you know the God we love says he will never leave you or walk out on you, right?" "Yes," I muttered between eye wipes. He went on. "You've been here before, and God has always led you to another job, right? I promise he won't let you down. He's always been faithful to me, and he's always been faithful to you."

As I stared at this beautiful man who emptied trash as he wore the label of janitor, I knew he was more than a custodian of a school; he was a custodian of faith, a faith that allowed Jesus to use him in remarkable ways. He was a trash-carrying disciple — available for hugs, discipline, and encouragement on the spot. The kind of disciple who loves Jesus from where he works, where he lives, and wherever he's stationed.

We don't have to change our surroundings to be a disciple. As a matter of fact, Jesus wants our surroundings *to be changed* by our love for him and our gratefulness for his grace. My husband, Bobby, is a baseball disciple. He breathes baseball. He dreams baseball. And it's inside the realm of baseball that God has put him to use. In an unlikely cathedral of infield dirt and grass, he is loving ballplayers and sharing truth and daring them to be men, to be lovers of the God who bestows athletic ability.

Moms on playgrounds, teachers in schools, attorneys in courtrooms, waitresses in restaurants, friends at Starbucks — all these settings provide the cathedrals in which disciples demonstrate love. A disciple is always thinking, "How can I show Christ here?" Sometimes it's with words, but mostly it's with love. Never fake or flurried, our demonstrations of love echo the words of our Master: "I came that they may have life, and have it abundantly" (John 10:10 NASB).

A Disciple's Transformation

It's tempting to look at people in the Bible and think they immediately "got it." To read about their Spirit hunger and assume they had a Disney

World-like "fast pass" ticket to a discipleship that we have to wait in line for. The truth is that they underwent a progression of growth and commitment, just like we have to. Moses hid for years before he saw a burning bush; Sarah laughed as she waited for a promised child; and Joseph spent time in a pit and prison before he ruled over a mass of people. Nothing delights me more than realizing I'm not on the dean's list of perennially slow learners — but rather I'm immersed in a sacred progression, the progression of being a disciple.

When Jesus began teaching in public, one of the first cities that heard his words was a city in Galilee named Capernaum. Populated by fishermen and farmers, Capernaum was the home of Peter, Andrew, James, John, Matthew — part of a formidable group of men who wore the badge of disciple. Before they wore badges, most of them simply fished. They went out on their boats, came back after a day of work, kissed wives, and went to the synagogue on the Sabbath.

It was at the synagogue that things began to get dicey. Jesus was preaching messages like nothing they had ever heard before. Peter's home was near the synagogue, so we can infer that he listened to Jesus on occasion before he personally had a relationship with him. All this changed when Jesus made a house visit to Peter's home after leaving the synagogue one day.

> Jesus left the synagogue and went to the home of Simon. Now Simon's mother-in-law was suffering from a high fever, and they asked Jesus to help her. So he bent over her and rebuked the fever, and it left her. She got up at once and began to wait on them.
>
> Luke 4:38 – 39

Although Peter has been listening to Jesus teach in a formal setting, their relationship is now progressing from friendly to personal. It's one thing to listen to Jesus preach periodically but quite another to have him walk into your home and heal a family member. I call this interpersonal connection "the intimacy circle."

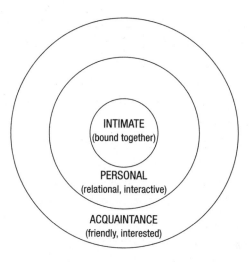

The circle starts with an *acquaintance*. We may feel an attraction to someone and be interested in knowing them better. It's not critical that we go further; we just find them appealing and wouldn't mind pursuing the relationship. The second stage of the circle is *personal*. This is the stage where we step into each other's lives. We've moved past acquaintance to caressing the joys and wounds of who we are. We share stories and prayer requests, and we break bread together. This is where Peter and Jesus were the day Jesus showed up to pray for Peter's sick mother-in-law. No longer acquaintances, Jesus has now entered the fray of Peter's life.

The final stage of the circle is the most coveted because it's here that we shift to the familiarity and affection that gives birth to *intimacy*. Peter has listened to Jesus from the pews. He has invited Jesus into his home. He has watched healing wash over his household, but he is about to experience an encounter with Jesus that will usher in an intimacy so profound that from here on out Peter will be called "disciple" — a student, an apprentice, a follower.

One day as Jesus was standing by the Lake of Gennesaret, the people were crowding around him and listening to the word of

God. He saw at the water's edge two boats, left there by the fishermen, who were washing their nets. He got into one of the boats, the one belonging to Simon, and asked him to put out a little from shore. Then he sat down and taught the people from the boat.

Luke 5:1 – 3

It's a bit odd to think that a crowd was listening to Jesus teach by the water, but Peter and his buddies weren't among them. They were off washing nets. So much for being spiritual! Their *livelihood* came before *lively change* as they chose nets over transformation. But Jesus had a plan as he intentionally targeted Peter's boat, wandered over to it, climbed into it, and asked him to push it out into the water so he could continue on with his message. He could have chosen any boat, but he picked Peter's. I suspect that Peter pushed the boat out and then may have jumped in with Jesus, now a captive audience with no dirty net to distract him.

When he had finished speaking, he said to Simon, "Put out into deep water, and let down the nets for a catch."

Simon answered, "Master, we've worked hard all night and haven't caught anything. But because you say so, I will let down the nets."

Luke 5:4 – 5

Although Peter and Jesus are rotating in the intimacy circle, Peter still doesn't know what Jesus is up to. After Jesus tells him to let down his nets in deep water, Peter respectfully, but with serious doubt written all over his face, informs him that they've already tried that. In other words, he's saying, "You're a great man and all, Jesus, but we know fish, and there just aren't any here!" Even the fact that he calls Jesus "Master" signals respect but not much in the way of intimacy.

Many people respect Jesus, but it doesn't mean they love him. I respect a lot of people I don't necessarily even like. I respect people I wouldn't follow into a business venture, much less give my life to. But for Peter, everything was about to change. With the gritty determination of a waitress who has no choice but to clean that dirty table before the next group can be seated, Peter decides to placate Jesus by heading out to the deep waters. Floating in the blue tide, Peter's nets became so full that the boat began to sink. In this instant, Peter moved from personal moments with a teacher to sacred intimacy with a Savior.

> When Simon Peter saw this, he fell at Jesus' knees and said, "Go away from me, Lord; I am a sinful man!" For he and all his companions were astonished at the catch of fish they had taken ... So they pulled their boats up on shore, left *everything* and followed him.
>
> Luke 5:8–9, 11, emphasis mine

Notice that it wasn't great teaching, amazing healings, or even wondrous miracles that pushed Peter to the ground in worship. It was Jesus acting on something that was fundamental to the lifeblood of who Peter was — catching fish.

Jesus still uses this path to intimacy with us today. He entices at the point of the needs and fears of our lives to fill our nets to capacity. Hurting relationships, shaky finances, personality quirks, troubled children, uncertain futures, loneliness, scars, setbacks — these are the nets he asks us to cast into the deep. If we're obedient, even in our reluctance (because we've tried that already and we know nothing else will work), we will have no trouble hauling in the catch. *He is that able.*

This is the path to intimacy. Jesus asks us to push out a bit so we can hear him teach us, and then he watches with a smile as we haul in a catch far beyond what we ever thought was possible.

A Disciple's Profile

To go from being believers *in* Christ to disciples *for* Christ is to shift toward a profound decision — to move from bystander to partaker, from fan to teammate.

At times I have whimpered, pointing out to God all the reasons he wouldn't want me on his team. But like a courageous captain picking a team on the playground, he continues to choose me.

I used to think I had to perform perfectly to play on God's team. Never fumbling or striking out. Always an all-star striving for peak performance. Now I realize it's the preparation, support, and guts I show my teammates that mean more to him than game-day accolades. It's the trust I have in his coaching decisions that shape my disciple-loving heart more than do stunning performances.

When we get in the game, we will display certain traits that will explain our behavior to those who observe. Characteristics that will identify our team as Christ's. One of the clearest attributes is this: *disciples act and react uniquely.*

During the last meal Jesus ate with his disciples before he went to the cross, he uttered words that must have had the men at the table scratching their beards.

"A new command I give you: Love one another. As I have loved you, so you must love one another. By this everyone will know that you are my disciples, if you love one another."

John 13:34 – 35

He didn't say they'll know us by our knowledge or by our perfect behavior. He said they'll know us *by our love.* This is fancy footwork for those of us who are apt to dance our way to discipleship with good works. It's not good works that leave tally marks to be counted by God; it's the aroma of love that ushers his scent all the way to heaven.

As we were growing up, my younger sister, Maureen, often bore the brunt of my short fuse. We had one car to share between my mom and us three kids — and we kids all fended for ourselves, which could mean either walking miles to our destination or lobbying to use the car. One night I won the coveted keys, and I planned to use the car to go meet some friends. There was only one catch. I had to pick up my sister from ballet class on the other side of town and deliver her back home before I could go.

Figuring I may have some time to kill as I waited, I threw my Bible on the front seat of our worn Chevy Nova and headed to the dance studio. After waiting for about fifteen minutes, I peered in the window, expecting to see the dancers exiting the room. Instead, it looked as though the class was just beginning. It didn't take me long to realize I would be waiting outside for at least another hour, and since this was before the days of cell phones, meeting up with my friends just wasn't going to happen.

I grabbed the Bible I had placed on the front seat and decided to use my time wisely. After about an hour, I saw my little sister slink her way toward the car, convinced she would receive the wrath of Gari once she opened the door and climbed in. Instead, I asked her how her class had gone. "I'm so sorry, Gar," she blurted. "I got the time wrong and couldn't slip out of class to tell you." I calmly assured her it was OK. She looked at me with a face that twisted sideways as I put the Bible down and turned the key to start the car. Up until this point she hadn't been sure what to make of my newfound faith. I was a lot of talk, but she needed to see action. She smiled a slow smile — the kind that starts with a crease and then invades the entire face — as she sighed. "Now I know your faith is real, Gari. The old you would have screamed at me for twenty minutes, while the new you says you're happy you could use the time to read. That's a miracle!" I don't always get it right, but that night I did, and it made a difference for my sister.

Loving God with abandon means loving others in unpredictable ways, and God is always looking for ways to show off this love within us. Corrie ten Boom tells a story that defies logic. Her actions push the boundaries of incomprehensible love and extravagant forgiveness.

After her release from a German concentration camp, Corrie traveled the world to share her story of faith and forgiveness. But in 1947, she had an encounter that shook her to the core just moments after she concluded her message in a church in a bombed-out, bitter Germany.

Speaking to the dark-eyed, solemn crowd, she used a vivid image to paint a picture of God's vast forgiveness. She told them that when they confess their sins, God casts them into the deepest ocean so they are gone forever. The people blankly stared at her as she finished talking. They silently filed out of the basement room. No questions, no pleasant exchanges — they simply picked up their coats and quietly began leaving.

And that's when I saw him, working his way forward against the others. One moment I saw the overcoat and brown hat; the next, a blue uniform and a visored cap with its skull and crossbones. It came back with a rush: the huge room with its harsh overhead lights; the pathetic pile of dresses and shoes in the center of the floor; the shame of walking naked past this man. I could see my sister's frail form ahead of me, ribs sharp beneath the parchment skin. *Betsie, how thin you were!*

[Betsie and I had been arrested for concealing Jews in our home during the Nazi occupation of Holland; and this man had been a guard at Ravensbruck concentration camp where we were sent.]

Now he was in front of me, hand thrust out: "A fine message, Fräulein! How good it is to know that, as you say, all our sins are at the bottom of the sea!"

And I, who had spoke so glibly of forgiveness, fumbled in my pocketbook rather than take that hand. He would not remember me, of course — how could he remember one prisoner among those thousands of women?

But I remembered him and the leather crop swinging from his belt. I was face-to-face with one of my captors and my blood seemed to freeze.

"You mentioned Ravensbruck in your talk," he was saying. "I was a guard there." No, he did not remember me.

"But since that time," he went on, "I have become a Christian. I know that God has forgiven me for the cruel things I did there, but I would like to hear it from your lips as well. Fräulein," — again the hand came out — "will you forgive me?"

And I stood there — I whose sins had again and again to be forgiven — and could not forgive. Betsie had died in that place — could he erase her slow, terrible death simply for the asking? …

I stood there with the coldness clutching my heart. But forgiveness is not an emotion — I knew that too. Forgiveness is an act of the will, and the will can function regardless of the temperature of the heart. "Help!" I prayed silently. "I can lift my hand. I can do that much. You supply the feeling."

And so woodenly, mechanically, I thrust my hand into the one stretched out to me. And as I did, an incredible thing took place. The current started in my shoulder, raced down my arm, sprang into our joined hands. And then this healing warmth seemed to flood my whole being, bringing tears to my eyes.

"I forgive you, brother!" I cried. "With all my heart!"

For a long moment we grasped each other's hands, the former guard and the former prisoner. I had never known God's love so intensely, as I did then.[26]

Like balm to an aching life, could Corrie withhold such a gift because her life bore the pain? Would her Savior withhold such a balm? She reached out to this man and uttered, "I forgive you," and in that instant heaven sang the grandeur of a disciple willing to love.

Unpredictable and unexplainable are the ways of a true disciple who acts and reacts in ways that alter the foundation of love.

Moving toward Opportunity

True disciples run toward opportunity, not away from it. The apostle Peter didn't settle down into a lucrative fishing business after encountering Jesus. His life goals and purpose shifted to a greater call — fishing for men and women. In the days of the early church, it was Peter who was the mouthpiece for the fledgling new believers. More apt to put his foot in his mouth than to be a mouthpiece, this pioneer struck out to mine spiritual gold. On the Day of Pentecost, it was gutsy Peter who spoke for the church when everyone around them thought they were drunk.

> Then Peter stood up with the Eleven, raised his voice and addressed the crowd: "Fellow Jews and all of you who live in Jerusalem, let me explain this to you; listen carefully to what I say. These people are not drunk, as you suppose. It's only nine in the morning! No, this is what was spoken by the prophet Joel ..."
>
> Acts 2:14 – 16

Peter goes on to deliver a sermon that could light wet branches on fire. Remembering that only a handful of time had passed since he cowered in denial of his Lord, it's a remarkable showdown — and all because he refused to crawl away from opportunity but chose to be empowered by it. That day three thousand people accepted his message and were baptized (Acts 2:41).

Peter ruffled the religious folks' feathers with his teaching. They are described as "greatly disturbed" (Acts 4:2) after hearing Peter's teaching about Jesus' resurrection. He also had them pondering how a man of little education, a smelly fisherman, to be exact, could speak such words of wisdom and eloquence.

> Now as they observed the confidence of Peter and John and understood that they were uneducated and untrained men, they were amazed, and began to recognize them as having been with Jesus.
>
> Acts 4:13 NASB

To be recognized as having been with Jesus is the brand I want stamped to the endorsement of my life. I'm not a fan of labels, but I am a fan of Christ. It doesn't matter how educated or trained we are, if we move toward opportunity rather than shy away from it, God uses our humble offering to bring hope to weary life travelers.

Setting Priorities

A disciple is willing to prioritize. I find my spiritual muscles beginning to quiver as I think about this. Can I please God and remain in good standing with my family, friends, coworkers, and acquaintances? Being the queen of people-pleasing, I certainly have tried. The truth is that I sometime make choices that will not please everyone but will decidedly please God. A disciple understands that these choices will arise and is willing to make them. Jesus offers some tough words in the process of picturing the priorities of his followers.

> "If anyone comes to me and does not hate father and mother, wife and children, brothers and sisters — yes, even their own life — such a person cannot be my disciple. And whoever does not carry their cross and follow me cannot be my disciple."
>
> Luke 14:26 – 27

The word in this passage that gives me pause is *hate*. Are we supposed to hate the very people we love? A deeper study of the word reveals that the implied meaning is "hate in comparison to your love for me." Now that I can swallow!

When I fell in love with my husband, I didn't notice his skin color; I adored his soul. One day as we held hands, I commented on how I loved the caramel color of his skin, different from the vanilla tone of my own hands. Bobby had told me stories of growing up in southern California, and although it was beyond the decades of blatant prejudice, he still hadn't been allowed to take the girl he really wanted to take to the prom. His date for the night was compelled to lie to her parents and tell them she was checking coats at the door as Bobby drove his father's Cadillac to meet her at a location other than her home.

Bobby seemed to know there would be trouble in paradise if we moved forward in our relationship, but I simply couldn't grasp why. After our engagement, I was stunned by my grandparents' reaction. My grandmother chided, "Honey, bluebirds should stay with bluebirds, and ravens with ravens." I guess I was the bluebird. Her approval meant the world to me, but I knew this man was part of God's plan for my life — so approval or no approval, I made the choice to marry him. I think this is what Jesus is getting at when he teaches that we have to care more about his approval than about the approval of those we love.

Oswald Chambers describes this predicament as he explains what it means to build for eternity:

> The conditions of discipleship laid down by our Lord mean that the men and women he is going to use in his mighty building enterprises are those in whom he has done everything. "If any man comes to me, and hate not ..., *he cannot be my disciple.*" Our Lord implies that the only men and women he will use in his building enterprises are those who love him personally, passionately, and devotedly beyond any of the closest ties on earth. The conditions are stern, but they are glorious.[27]

These words may leave us feeling a bit uncomfortable, but I've come to realize that if I'm not feeling a bit uncomfortable a few times a year, I'm probably not growing as a disciple. Our priority isn't to get more comfortable; it is to be so in love with God that we cannot separate our desires from his.

Oh, the depth of this mystery — the sheer elation of running with a Savior who can't be outrun! Like a kite that blows in the currents of the wind, so are disciples of the living Christ.

> "The wind blows where it wishes and you hear the sound of it, but do not know where it comes from and where it is going, so is everyone who is born of the Spirit."

John 3:8 NASB

My uncle used to buy us colorful kites to fly as we ran along the sandy beaches of the shore. It was hard work to get them in the air. I would run and fall, rolling in a tangled heap as he shouted, "Keep going; you're almost flying!"

Spirit hunger is a lot like kite flying: If we are willing to get in the air, we'll be carried by the Spirit's current, which is more than able to sustain us. We don't need to be afraid of the wind of the Spirit; instead, we can fly in it. For with this sure hope, our Spirit hunger will find wings of its own, and soar.

a note from gari

Sweet Friends,

I hate good-byes! I'll do anything to get around them. So it is with pleasure that I invite you to go further with me — continuing our journey with prayer and belief. Would you consider spending time in the DVD Bible study with workbook titled *Spirit Hunger*?

It's a place where we can romp and roam as we look more closely at engaging God. There will be plenty of room for writing, pondering, and digging in. I hope you'll come along!

I love to hear from readers and interact with you. Please feel free to drop by my website (www.garimeacham.com) or follow my blog (www.trulyfed.blogspot.com). Please know that I am praying for you with a joy that is deep and real.

With much love,
Gari

NOTES

1. John and Stasi Eldredge, *Captivating: Unlocking the Mystery of a Woman's Soul* (Nashville: Nelson, 2005).
2. See Eldredge and Eldredge, *Captivating*, 23.
3. Richard Foster, *Prayer: Finding the Heart's True Home* (San Francisco: HarperSanFrancisco, 1992), 3.
4. Ibid., 3 – 4.
5. Tricia McCary Rhodes, *The Soul at Rest: A Journey into Contemplative Prayer* (Minneapolis: Bethany House, 1996), 28.
6. Oswald Chambers, *My Utmost for His Highest* (Ulrichsville, Ohio: Barbour, 2000), 103.
7. Oswald Chambers, *My Utmost for His Highest* (Ulrichsville, Ohio: Barbour, 2000), 37.
8. Oswald Chambers, *My Utmost for His Highest* (Ulrichsville, Ohio: Barbour, 2000), 105.
9. See Richard Foster, *Prayer: Finding the Heart's True Home* (San Francisco: HarperSanFrancisco, 1992), 123.
10. "Introduction to James," *Life Application Bible* (Wheaton, Ill.: Tyndale House, 1988), 1915.
11. *Life Application Bible*, 1917.
12. See Gari Meacham, *Truly Fed: Finding Freedom from Disordered Eating* (Kansas City, Mo.: Beacon Hill, 2009), 132.
13. Oswald Chambers, *My Utmost for His Highest* (Ulrichsville, Ohio: Barbour, 2000), 33.
14. Oswald Chambers, *My Utmost for His Highest* (Ulrichsville, Ohio: Barbour, 2000), 223.
15. Beth Moore, *Believing God* (Nashville: LifeWay, 2002), 7.

16. See Gari Meacham, *Truly Fed: Finding Freedom from Disordered Eating* (Kansas City: Beacon Hill, 2009), 149.

17. Larry Crabb, in a speech to a group of major league baseball wives at Coors Field in Denver, Colorado, in 1996.

18. Henri Nouwen, *Making All Things New* (New York: HarperCollins, 1981), 67–68.

19. Richard Foster, *Prayer: Finding the Heart's True Home* (San Francisco: HarperSanFrancisco, 1992), 191.

20. Oswald Chambers, *My Utmost for His Highest* (Ulrichsville, Ohio: Barbour, 2000), 63–64.

21. P. T. Forsyth, *The Soul of Prayer* (Grand Rapids: Eerdmans, 1916), 53.

22. Charles Stanley, *When the Enemy Strikes: The Keys to Winning Your Spiritual Battles* (Nashville: Nelson, 2004), 116.

23. Richard Foster, *Prayer: Finding the Heart's True Home* (San Francisco: HarperSanFrancisco, 1992), 197.

24. James MacDonald, *Downpour: He Will Come to Us Like the Rain* (Nashville: Broadman and Holman, 2006), 38.

25. Oswald Chambers, *My Utmost for His Highest* (Ulrichsville, Ohio: Barbour, 2000), 127.

26. Corrie ten Boom, "I'm Still Learning to Forgive," *Guideposts*, 1972, www.familylifeeducation.org/gilliland/procgroup/CorrieTenBoom.htm (accessed February 28, 2012).

27. Oswald Chambers, *My Utmost for His Highest* (Ulrichsville, Ohio: Barbour, 2000), 91.

Spirit Hunger Workbook with DVD

Filling Our Deep Longing to Connect with God

Gari Meacham

In this six-session video-based study with workbook, author and speaker Gari Meacham identifies the path we share as we struggle to engage God in prayer and belief.

Here, your heart's desire to engage God is unwrapped, and lesser loves are stripped away, until a unique fragrance of God—a scent that has either never been unveiled or has been ignored—is exposed in your heart.

Meacham writes, "With the authenticity of my own life stories— marriage to a professional baseball player, struggles with severe food bondage, and a father who was a quadriplegic—I came to the crisp realization that my prayer life and my level of belief needed to match. *Spirit Hunger* provides a clear path toward matching these heart cries— leading away from crumbs and counterfeit to a hungering for God."

Meacham offers a fresh look on the topic of prayer that will help you move past longings to settle in a place where you can authentically engage God.

This *Spirit Hunger* curriculum pack contains one *Spirit Hunger* participant's guide and one *Spirit Hunger* DVD.

Available in stores and online!

ZONDERVAN®
.com

Share Your Thoughts

With the Author: Your comments will be forwarded to the author when you send them to *zauthor@zondervan.com*.

With Zondervan: Submit your review of this book by writing to *zreview@zondervan.com*.

Free Online Resources at
www.zondervan.com

Zondervan AuthorTracker: Be notified whenever your favorite authors publish new books, go on tour, or post an update about what's happening in their lives at www.zondervan.com/authortracker.

Daily Bible Verses and Devotions: Enrich your life with daily Bible verses or devotions that help you start every morning focused on God. Visit www.zondervan.com/newsletters.

Free Email Publications: Sign up for newsletters on Christian living, academic resources, church ministry, fiction, children's resources, and more. Visit www.zondervan.com/newsletters.

Zondervan Bible Search: Find and compare Bible passages in a variety of translations at www.zondervanbiblesearch.com.

Other Benefits: Register to receive online benefits like coupons and special offers, or to participate in research.

ZONDERVAN®

ZONDERVAN.com/
AUTHORTRACKER
follow your favorite authors